This Book Will
Make You Feel
Beautiful

Dr Jessamy Hibberd
and
Jo Usmar

Quercus

ISBN 978-1-62365-676-8

Library of Congress Control Number: 2015955411

Distributed in the United States and Canada by
Hachette Book Group
1290 Avenue of the Americas
New York, NY 10104

Manufactured in the United States

10 9 8 7 6 5 4 3 2 1

www.quercus.com

Contents

A note from the authors

We live in ever-changing times and sometimes life can be tough. We're constantly being pulled in different directions and can struggle to cope with the pressure that we're put under by external factors and, most importantly, by ourselves. With greater choice comes greater responsibility and occasionally this can be a breeding ground for insecurity, unhappiness and self-doubt. There are very few people (if any at all) who feel they operate perfectly in their work, relationships and life in general. Most of us could use some help now and then – a nudge to show us how to improve our self-esteem, to change our approach to life and to feel more content. All too often we can feel we don't measure up, either to other people or to a mythical ideal we hold in our heads.

The *This Book Will* series aims to help you understand why you feel, think and behave the way you do and then gives you the tools to make positive changes. We're not fans of complicated medical jargon so we've tried to make everything accessible, relevant and entertaining as we know you'll want to see improvements as soon as possible. We draw on our professional experience and the latest research, using anecdotes and examples which we found helpful and hope you will too. Titles are split into particular subjects such as happiness, body image, mindfulness and stress, so you can focus on the areas you'd most like to address.

Our books are based on a Cognitive Behavioural Therapy (CBT) framework. CBT is an incredibly successful treatment for a wide variety of issues and we're convinced it will help you to cope with whatever you're facing.

Within all of our books you'll regularly come across diagrams called mind maps. We use these to illustrate how your thoughts, behaviour, mood and body are all connected. Filling these in will break any problem down so it doesn't seem overwhelming, while laying out options for making changes.

There are strategies and checklists throughout, to guide you through the practical steps of improving your body image and self-confidence. We'll make it easy for these changes to become part of your routine because reading the theory is only going to get you so far. The only way to start feeling beautiful is to put everything you learn into practice, changing how you feel about yourself and how you experience your day-to-day life.

You can choose to feel better and live life differently and this book will show you how.

Good luck! Let us know how you get on by contacting us on our website: www.jessamyandjo.com.

Jessamy and Jo

Introduction

You may have heard the phrase 'beauty is in the eye of the beholder' before and dismissed it as a well-meaning platitude to perk up someone feeling a bit insecure about their appearance. Well, what if you were the 'beholder' and the beauty in question was your own? In your own eyes, how do you measure up – do you consider yourself beautiful? How about reasonably good looking? Or average? Or even OK?

Chances are your answers are along the lines of: 'Well, I might be if I lost X amount of weight/had a different nose/got rid of this scar/didn't have acne.'

How you view yourself, how you see yourself physically, can affect your emotions, thoughts, behaviour and body. Needless to say, if your opinions are negative – if you don't feel you're up to scratch or believe you're lacking physically in some way – it can shape your whole world. That's not an exaggeration. Feeling insecure in your appearance can inhibit what you do, say, think and the choices you make.

Unfortunately, more and more people (both men and women) are feeling dissatisfied with how they look. Recent research found that 90 per cent of British women experience body image anxiety, 50 per cent of girls who smoke do so to suppress their appetites and 69 per cent of men 'often' wish they looked like someone else. These statistics should be shocking, but, sadly, they're not. Chances are you picked up this book because you suffer from physical insecurities that affect your life or you know someone else who does. Which, in a way, is sort of good news. No, really, it is – because it means you're not alone. Feeling low, insecure, angry, ashamed or embarrassed about how you look can be exceptionally lonely, but please be reassured that how you feel is a totally normal response to external and internal pressures. You're not bad, wrong or weird for feeling the way you do. Knowing other people are going through the same thing won't inspire any high-fives or merry jigs, but it should puncture the loneliness a bit.

Most of the views we hold about our appearance are unfair, unrealistic and unhelpful, but we've become so attached to them we consider them absolute truths. We *are* too ugly, fat, thin, scrawny, big, tall, short, hairy, bald or gangly. We dismiss anything that points to the contrary and only ever focus on totally nonsensical 'evidence' that backs up our views ('She's staring at the huge gap in my teeth', 'I didn't get the job because I don't look the part').

This brings us to the second bit of good news: there are loads of ways to combat these negative impressions and to create a much healthier and realistic view of yourself. By challenging these thoughts, changing your behaviour and actively pursuing a healthier body image you'll feel more confident, self-assured and happier with how you look and life in general. Which is where this book comes in.

Why choose this book?

If you want straightforward advice on how to feel happier and more confident in your appearance, then this is the book for you. There's no airy-fairy gibberish or whimsical fancy, just practical strategies that are proven to work, explained in a simple and, hopefully, fairly entertaining way, with relatable real life examples.

It can be alarmingly easy to accept body image anxiety as a permanent fixture in your life, but that's an awful plan. Believing you're not attractive enough or that you have an inescapable physical flaw can be hugely debilitating because your body is with you forever – you can't swap it or shape-shift like an alien. Everyone suffers from insecurities about their appearance sometimes – everyone. Yes, even that supermodel living next door. Having occasional worries is totally natural – it's when those thoughts start to dictate your decisions that something needs to change.

Learning to accept and, yes, even appreciate the body you've got will do wonders for your self-esteem and your confidence in other areas of your life too.

How it all works

This is a manual on how to battle body image demons and how to feel more beautiful. That means you're actually going to have to try the strategies and techniques we suggest, investing time and energy into them. There's no point skim-reading everything and thinking, 'Well, I still hate my ears'. Of course you do! You'll only alter ingrained thinking and behavioural patterns by actively trying to alter them.

We'll be using a Cognitive Behavioural Therapy (CBT) framework, which is explained in more detail in Chapter 2. Focused on problem-solving, it's a brilliant and highly effective approach to dealing with any difficulties you may be experiencing in the here and now. It will allow you to break issues down in simple ways so they become less all-consuming and more manageable. The tools CBT will give you are for life, there's no time limit, so you can use them whenever you need to.

How to get the most out of this book

+ Read the chapters in numerical order as each one builds on the last. Once you've got the hang of it you'll be able to dip in and out as you need
+ Try all of the strategies rather than just picking and choosing (the strategies are all identified by ⓢ). They are proven to work – we're not asking you to do them just for a laugh. You might be surprised at which ones work for you and which ones you're good at. By trying them all you'll be giving yourself a better chance at improving your body image long-term

✦ Practise! Old habits are hard to break and many of the beliefs you have about how you look, and behaviours associated with those beliefs, have been built up over years and years. You'll need to practise to ensure your new ways of thinking and acting become second nature. Some of what we recommend may be tough, uncomfortable or strange to you, but don't be discouraged. Keep at it and you'll soon see results

✦ Buy a new notebook and dedicate it to this book. We'll be asking you to note things down or draw things out and this is an integral part of the process. Writing things down aids memory and makes things more 'official' in your own head. Also, it'll be really motivational to flick through previous notes and see how far you've come

Feeling bad about how you look shouldn't limit what you do in life or clog up all your headspace. You absolutely can and will feel more confident and happy with your appearance if you really invest time and energy in changing how you view yourself, no matter how long you've felt insecure or what's happened to you in the past. Just by picking up this book you are making a positive statement of intent: I want to feel better, I want to accept myself and I will.

I

Why Do We Hate the Way We Look?

Why are so many of us consumed by how we look? How do these thoughts affect our lives? This chapter examines the root causes of body image insecurities so you're in a better place to start tackling them.

Uncomfortable in our skin

The *Oxford English Dictionary* defines 'beautiful' as 'very attractive' and 'attractiveness' as 'pleasing or appealing to the senses'. But who or what decides whether you qualify? Let's get this straight from the start – it is an unarguable fact that different people find different things beautiful and/or sexy. There is no 'right' way to look. What people are physically drawn to is shaped by their childhood, their cultural background, their friends and families, popular culture and their own personal desires. However, it is another unarguable fact that a general consensus can be formed within different countries, cultures and societal groups that says looking a certain way is desirable, be it short, tall, skinny, curvaceous, pale, dark, heavy, athletic, hairy or hairless. And these generally accepted beliefs fuel body image anxieties.

What is body image?

'Body image' refers to the beliefs you have about your physical appearance. It's your internalised view of yourself – how you look to yourself and how you imagine you look to other people. It includes:

✦ How you perceive your body visually
✦ How you think and talk about your body
✦ Your sense of how other people view your body
✦ Your sense of your body in physical space ('I'm taking up too much room')
✦ Your level of connectedness to your body, i.e. whether you feel your body is a key part of 'you' (yourself as a person) or merely a vessel that gets you from A to B

Body image can be positive, negative or somewhere in the middle. It can also vary over time in response to a life event or a dramatic change in your physicality (for example, having a baby, becoming ill, having an accident, or putting on/losing lots of weight).

When you have a realistic perception of your body, you're more likely to have a positive body image. When what you think you look like matches how you actually appear to others, your body image tends to be positive because you're not harbouring unrealistic fixations on so-called 'flaws'.

Do you have body image anxieties?

Ask yourself the following questions:

1 Do I spend a great deal of time focused on one particular aspect of my appearance ('I hate my big forehead')?
2 Do I feel this part of my body is flawed in some way and that it needs to change to become acceptable ('I need to do lots of sit-ups to tone my flabby stomach')?
3 Do I make an effort to hide this 'flaw'? Do I constantly think about how to improve it?
4 Do others try to reassure me that I look fine (though I find it hard to believe them)?
5 Have I considered surgery?

If you answered yes to any of the above questions, you may be experiencing body image problems. It's important to keep in mind, though, that caring about how you look isn't bad. It's very rare to meet someone who couldn't care less about their appearance. Looking after your body is a key part of feeling good about yourself both emotionally and physically. We all feel insecure about our appearance at times; it's completely natural. However, it's when this insecurity becomes permanent and all-consuming that things need to change.

Negative body image can inspire distorted perceptions of size, shape and 'acceptability', both subjectively (how you see yourself) and objectively (how you believe others see you). People with negative body image tend to feel their physical 'flaws' are a sign of personal failure and a symptom or cause of unhappiness in their life ('Everything would be better if I was thin'). Their physical self is intrinsically tied up in self-worth and they can end up putting themselves down in all aspects of life because of it.

Here are common areas of fixation for people with body image issues:

+ Facial features: nose, eyes, eyebrows, lashes, hair, ears, mouth, teeth or lips
+ Face shape
+ Weight: feeling you're too fat or too thin
+ Muscles/build: believing you're too flabby, not toned enough, overly well-built or not well-built enough
+ Skin: acne, spots, wrinkles, stretch-marks, moles or uneven complexion
+ Hair: thinning or excessive hair on the head or body
+ Genitals: you worry they're too big, too small or the 'wrong' shape
+ Particular areas of the body: stomach, breasts, buttocks, arms, legs, hands, feet, neck
+ Body symmetry: feeling your body is unbalanced or lop-sided
+ Scars on the face or body
+ Height: believing you're too short or too tall

Preoccupations with body image can affect your day-to-day life, leading to unhelpful and distressing behaviours that only exacerbate your fears, such as controlling your diet, using heavy make-up, constantly checking your reflection or defensive body language. (We explain these behaviours and how to combat them in Chapter 3.) All of these take up huge amounts of time and headspace, having an impact on:

+ Family, social and romantic relationships: you avoid going out if you feel you don't 'look your best'; you compare yourself to friends and so feel insecure when you're with them; worrying about your body distracts you from the outside world; you avoid starting new relationships through fear of judgement; you worry about appearing vain or superficial so don't talk about your anxieties; you dismiss compliments; you believe people don't or won't understand your fears

+ Work or study: time you spend worrying, checking, grooming eats into time that should be spent working/studying – everything takes longer

+ Confidence: being constantly focused on your perceived physical defects can shatter your self-esteem, leaving you feeling low, anxious, ashamed, sexually inhibited or possibly even depressed

+ Your wallet: you may spend lots of money on beauty treatments, clothes or cosmetic procedures

+ Food and diet: food can play a huge role in your life, socially and personally. You may have your own personal rules for success and failure when it comes to diet (see Chapter 5)

+ Exercise: you may exercise excessively, prioritising it over social events, punishing yourself if you mess up your fitness schedule. Alternatively, you may avoid exercise, but feel guilty or ashamed about this

We address all of these things in this book, with simple strategies to start changing negative thinking and behavioural patterns to more positive ones.

Body dysmorphia disorder (BDD)

BDD is a body image anxiety disorder characterised by intense preoccupation (or obsession) with a perceived flaw in appearance. Sufferers' concerns about this flaw will drastically affect their life and can result in compulsive behaviours and routines (closely related to obsessive compulsive disorder/OCD) such as excessive use of mirrors, skin-picking, withdrawing socially, covering up flaws (with clothes, make-up or hands), spending hours getting ready to go out, changing outfits repeatedly and making constant comparisons with others. It can lead to depression, anxiety, shame, guilt and loneliness, misuse of alcohol and/or drugs, self-harm and even suicidal thoughts.

> ⋯∴ Approximately 1–2 per cent of the population will be experiencing BDD at any one time and it affects both men and women equally. However, it's hard to track because sufferers don't tend to seek help, not recognising it as a psychological problem, instead believing there really is something wrong with their body.
>
> If you believe you might be suffering from BDD please see your GP as well as continuing with this book. The strategies we recommend will complement more specialist treatment.

Beauty is a social and cultural construct, meaning the parameters for physical attractiveness vary greatly according to the current era and trends. So, taking on board the fact we're all different and are attracted to different things, why do so many of us dislike or, yes, even hate, the way we look?

What and who decides whether we're beautiful?
Our visual culture
Trends come and go, but when the media, the fashion industry and advertisers latch onto a certain look, or when a celebrity comes along who captures the collective imagination, it affects us all. Now more than ever we live in a visual culture. Whereas in previous centuries you'd only be aware of the 'beauty ideal' if you had access to poetry, theatre or art, nowadays pictures of what's deemed to be physically aspirational are unavoidable. Even if you hid in a cave for a month you'd inevitably find a tatty old gossip mag to flick through with snaps of 'CELEBS LOOKING FABULOUS!' splashed across the cover.

Advances in technology, instant access to the internet, advertising and social media ensure we spend our lives digesting countless images of what is considered currently 'beautiful' whether we want to or not: that guy looking moody on the perfume advert, the woman in a bikini pointing at the sunset, the kid with the blindingly white teeth eating a yoghurt. While we've become savvier about media manipulations, this doesn't mean they don't work their way under our skin. Yes, we can recognise when an image has been edited or 'photoshopped', but then you're left asking why.

We're also encouraged to live our own lives online via photographs and constant status updates on social media sites, which can aggravate existing feelings of insecurity.

Normalisation of plastic surgery

Lunchtime Lipo! Divorce Pick-Me-Up Nose Jobs! Through media stories, celebrity endorsements and TV make-over shows, plastic surgery has become normalised when it's actually a pretty drastic method of 'physical betterment'. It's now viewed as a viable and affordable option for those with physical anxieties. While many surgeries do offer comprehensive psychological evaluations before allowing new patients to undergo treatment, sadly many places don't. Many people desperately low in confidence and self-esteem are trying to 'fix' their insecurities through surgery, rather than investigating the far more important issue of why they feel the way they do about their body.

Fad diets

We discuss fad diets (and why they don't work!) in depth in Chapter 5, but for now suffice to say that the very fact diets are so popular proves how they're both driven by people's desire to look different and at the same time perpetuate the self-doubt cycle. The more you focus negatively on your body, the worse you feel about it. You're told that change is achievable and so if you can't, or don't, achieve it you feel like a failure and quickly turn to the next diet or 'quick fix'. These patterns of thoughts and behaviour can turn into a vicious circle (see overleaf).

Feel worried or insecure about how you look

Think 'life would be better/easier/more satisfying if I changed X,Y or Z'

Seek out articles/books/ pictures/diets/surgery that seemingly 'prove' your insecurity ('See? There *is* something wrong')

Try the miracle cure or 'quick fix' and when/if it doesn't deliver move onto the next one

Fictional heroes (television, film and books)

As a kid you no doubt rooted for the stunning princesses and charming princes over the ugly witches. In films, beautiful women and dashing heroes rule the day, while villains are often ugly or disfigured. Also, while things are gradually changing, accusations of ageism have been rife in the television and film industries for years, aggravating our fear of getting older – that we should avoid it or try to reverse it at all costs.

Childhood beliefs

If Barbie were life-sized she'd have a 76 per cent healthy body weight, that is, she'd be in hospital. Yet, why wouldn't you believe Barbie's perfect when she has such a great life and gorgeous man-friend, Ken? Why wouldn't you associate beauty with good and ugly with evil when that's what all the fairy tales say? Why wouldn't you think fashion models and shop-front mannequins have ideal figures when they're all over the high street? (Just so you know: if standard-sized mannequins were real women they'd be too thin to be able to bear children.)

When you grow up you accept what you're told because you have no basis for comparison. Our beliefs and impressions of the world and our view of ourselves and others are formed and developed in childhood. These beliefs tend to be centred around ideas of self-worth, achievement, acceptance and lovability. At five years of age children begin to recognise judgements, right and wrong, what's considered acceptable and what isn't. By seven years of age, they begin to show body dissatisfaction. And then come the teenage years – a minefield of potential insecurities – when bodies change, develop and sexual attraction starts.

If your parents or friends had body image insecurities themselves and/ or had a disordered relationship with food, this will have affected how you viewed appearance, food and mealtimes as you grew up. Similarly, if you were ever teased about your appearance it might have instigated beliefs that will have affected your adulthood self-esteem. One negative comment can haunt you for years: 'She's got a horrible double chin', 'His eyes are too close together'. These opinions can turn into facts in your mind ('My double chin is horrible', 'My eyes do look weird') and form the basis of beliefs you hold about yourself.

Self-deprecation and 'fat talk'

Everything we've mentioned so far contributes to a belief that a certain way of looking is 'good' and another way of looking is 'bad'. This can lead to an assumption that you should apologise for how you look – that you need to acknowledge your faults before anyone else can: 'I shouldn't have eaten that' or 'I can't wear my hair up because of my ears'. People can also make excuses for other people's appearance: 'You wear a Large? Well, that's only because you've got great boobs.' This assumption that wearing a large size needs excusing in some way fuels the idea of a 'thin ideal', the same way that a compliment like, 'You look great, have you lost weight?' does, equating weight loss with success and attractiveness.

This is what's called 'fat talk': statements made in conversation that reinforce unfair, unrealistic beauty ideals, inviting comparisons and aggravating body image anxieties. The Centre for Appearance Research (CAR) at University of the West of England found that after three minutes of 'fat talk', people's body dissatisfaction increased significantly.

Survival of the fittest

When we lived in caves, wearing woolly mammoth-skin skirts, our prehistoric brains were focused on finding a mate, belonging to a community and 'fitting in'. Losing the protection of your tribe was a life-or-death situation. We may have fancier homes and clothes nowadays, but those same concerns still drive us. Our fear of rejection and desire to belong fuels body image anxieties. It taps into our survival-of-the-fittest psyche, making us compare ourselves to others to see how we measure up.

Stress and unhappiness

Your appearance can become the focus of your attention if you're feeling under pressure or are unhappy in other aspects of your life. If you're emotionally distressed your body becomes an easy focus because it's always there and you can control how you treat it. It's easy to start thinking 'Life would be better if I was more attractive', but your quests for physical perfection won't fix things, because you're not dealing with the real underlying issue (i.e. a stressful job, a family problem, a disagreement with a friend or a health issue). As long as that problem remains you'll just keep moving the goalposts regarding your appearance ('I've lost half a stone and still feel rubbish – if I lose another half stone I'll feel better').

The thing we all forget about 'attractiveness'

Appearance matters and there's no point pretending it doesn't. How you represent yourself physically is the first account of yourself you give when meeting new people. However, it's not just your physical appearance that people are drawn to. We can get so caught up in how we look that we forget we're a whole package. You could look like a Greek god or goddess, but if you're rude and obnoxious you may tick the 'visual' attractiveness box, but you'll get big fat crosses everywhere else.

Attractiveness incorporates all of the below as well as appearance:

+ Manner (polite, shy, quiet, loud, out-going or introverted)
+ Style (clothes, haircut, make-up, jewellery and tattoos)
+ Confidence (whether you appear self-assured, happy within yourself)
+ Character and personality
+ Body language (defensive or 'open')
+ Sense of humour
+ Intelligence

In a culture fixated on looks, these things often get forgotten or relegated to the 'less-important' pile, but what you think about someone's physical attractiveness changes as you get to know them. Someone who might not be considered 'conventionally' attractive can become incredibly so when you're laughing at their thigh-slapping jokes. In the same way someone you wouldn't normally fancy can inspire an all-encompassing infatuation when you realise how kind, generous and confident they are.

It's human nature to want to be the best you can be and appearance plays a big part. People want to look their best and why shouldn't they? However, when thoughts and worries about appearance take up all your headspace and curb your enjoyment of life, it's time to take action. If your dreams for a better life centre on improving your appearance you'll never fully appreciate what you have and what's happening now.

Your life is being damaged not by your appearance, but by the way you feel about it. Research shows the way someone feels about their looks has a far greater effect on their quality of life than how they actually look. For example, you may feel the mole on your face is ruining your life when in reality no one else cares at all (no offence). Recognising this difference (how you look versus how you feel about how you look) is the first step to feeling more beautiful. Your body's not holding you back; how you feel about it is. You can change unhelpful, destructive thoughts and behaviours so you feel happier, more content and at peace with your body and therefore life in general. Your appearance shouldn't define who you are; the strategies in this book will ensure it doesn't.

⑤ Why do I want to feel beautiful?

In your notebook write down your answers to this question. (Writing down your answers is crucial. It's all too easy to think, 'I'll just remember them' – you won't. Give these answers the attention they deserve.)

Here are some ideas to help you consider your motivations. I want to feel beautiful because:

+ I want to feel more confident socially/at work/in my relationship
+ I want to feel good about myself and within myself
+ I want to feel more energetic rather than lethargic and sluggish
+ I want to feel happier
+ I want to accept myself and stop feeling that I need to change
+ I want a healthy sex life/I don't want to be scared of sex
+ I want to stop going on diets/obsessing over food
+ I want to stop comparing myself to everyone else
+ I want to stop feeling I'm not good enough
+ I want to feel excited about life
+ I want to wear clothes I like, rather than ones I feel I should wear
+ I want to be less self-conscious

✦ I want to feel more in control
✦ I want to do all the things I keep putting off through insecurity

Once you've completed your list type it up and print it out, pin it on the fridge, stick it to your mirror or on the inside cover of this book! The more places you have it the better. Set a time to read it every day. Put a reminder on your phone or write it in your diary so you don't forget. Read it whenever you're struggling with self-critical or negative thoughts or when you fall back into old habits.

Review: This strategy is key to fighting fears or insecurities that may appear during the course of this book. You're doing something new and battling thoughts, beliefs and behaviours that have been entrenched for years. Sometimes you may want to give up and go back to where you feel 'safe'— hating your weight/nose/legs or going on another diet. Whenever you feel that way, look at this list and remind yourself why you're doing this and all the things you have to gain by feeling good about yourself.

Thoughts to take away

✓ Your looks do not define you

✓ Fostering a healthier body image by challenging negative thoughts and behaviours will make you feel more confident in all aspects of your life

✓ Writing down your reasons for wanting to feel beautiful will motivate you whenever you slip into old, unhelpful patterns

2

Cognitive Behavioural Therapy

An explanation of CBT and why it's so brilliant at tackling body image issues. Here we start you off thinking about how your thoughts, behaviour, body and mood are all connected and how you can stop habitual negative patterns.

What is CBT?

Cognitive Behavioural Therapy (CBT) may sound like something practised in Area 51 by shady government officials, but there's absolutely nothing to be wary of. It's a leading treatment for all kinds of mental health issues and yes, body image anxiety can be classed as a mental health issue. There's a stigma attached to the phrase 'mental health' that's complete nonsense – it simply means looking after what's going on inside your head. Insecurity over appearance and preoccupations with food can affect your life, sap you of energy and crush your self-esteem. It's all very well someone telling you to 'pull yourself together' or advising you to keep your chin up, but when it comes to feeling better, advice like that is about as useful as an inflatable dartboard. But fear not, for this is where CBT comes in.

Pioneered by Dr Aaron T. Beck in the 1960s, CBT is recommended by the National Institute of Clinical Excellence (NICE) as a highly effective treatment for a wide variety of disorders – everything from stress and anxiety to insomnia, anorexia nervosa and bulimia. And there's no magic mumbo-jumbo involved, it's been rigorously tested and it works. It's all about finding practical strategies to cope with whatever life throws at you and once you've learned them you'll have them for life.

CBT is based on the belief that it's not what happens that affects you; it's how you interpret what happens. Your thoughts about a situation will affect your body, your behaviour and your mood. We actively construct the meaning of what goes on around us and then act on it.

How to understand body image using CBT

If you think you have a problem with the way you look, this will affect your emotions (you might worry about your appearance), your physicality (you may tense up/feel sick) and your behaviour (you might start a new diet or pore over photos of yourself, analysing 'flaws'). Your thoughts, mood, body and behaviour are all interlinked.

Here's an example to show you what we mean:

Fiona's 20-a-day habit

Fiona worked at home for three days a week as part of her company's flexi-hours scheme. After six months she noticed she'd put on a considerable amount of weight. She started to take note of her eating habits and realised that whenever she received a stressful email or phone call, she'd go to make herself a cup of tea and open the fridge to find a snack while the kettle boiled. She did it on autopilot, without thinking. The kitchen in her house was synonymous with cooking and eating, so as soon as she walked in her mind switched to food and she'd open the fridge.

Now she knew she was doing it, she thought she'd be able to stop, or at least cut down, on her snacking. But she didn't. She looked forward to her snack breaks more than anything else in the day. One day she realised she'd eaten 20 chocolate-digestive biscuits when she reached for another and the packet was empty. She started to feel embarrassed and guilty about her secret snacking and disgusted with her weight gain. She also felt like a failure for not having more self-control.

We can show what happened to Fiona in a snazzy diagram called a 'mind map' (see overleaf), showing how your thoughts, behaviour, emotions and body (physicality) are all linked.

Fiona's snacking habit mind map would look like this:

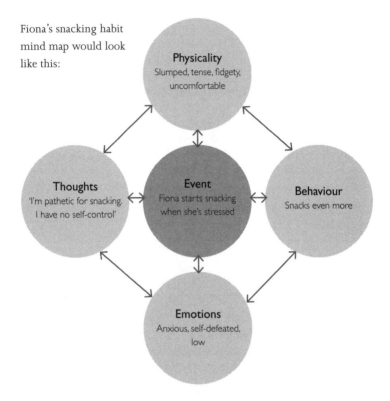

Physicality
Slumped, tense, fidgety, uncomfortable

Event
Fiona starts snacking when she's stressed

Thoughts
'I'm pathetic for snacking. I have no self-control'

Behaviour
Snacks even more

Emotions
Anxious, self-defeated, low

These thought-body-mood-behaviour connections form the basis of CBT. If one of the sections is negative it will affect all the rest, much like falling dominoes.

By filling out a mind map Fiona can break down what's happening and see how her thoughts are both triggering and, in turn, being triggered by her snacking (behaviour), low mood and slumped, tense physicality. By breaking things down in this way, she's giving herself options to make changes. She can ask herself: 'Am I really snacking because I have no self-control or because I'm unhappy with work? Is thinking this way helping or making things worse? Is the additional stress I'm putting myself under by worrying about my weight aggravating the problem?' She can then work to change each section of the mind map by altering her interpretation of what's happening, changing her behaviour and calming down her body – all of which will have a positive knock-on effect on her mood. If she does that, her mind map would look like this instead:

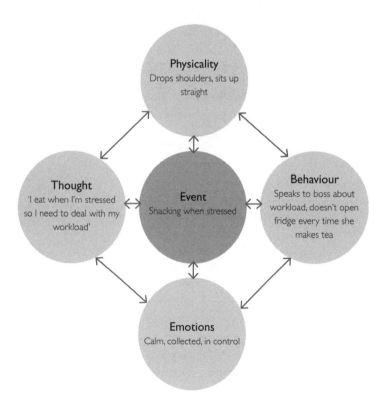

Your interpretations are shaped by the situation, long-held beliefs and how you feel at the time. CBT teaches you how to take note of your thoughts, body, behaviour and mood so you can begin to see habitual negative patterns and learn how to stop or change them.

Here are some example thoughts (interpretations) about what can happen when you feel overdressed at an event:

'These things always happen to me' → depressed

'I'm going to fall over in these heels and hurt myself' → anxious

'What an absolute IDIOT I am' → angry

'Hey, at least I'm not naked' → calm

Clearly the last one is going to make your head a better place to live in, so why does your mind always default to the others?

Preoccupation

Body image anxieties can make you preoccupied with how you look and/or with food. Your thoughts and behaviours (for example, checking mirrors, pictures of yourself on Facebook or reading up on diets) feed this preoccupation, which in turn provokes *more* negative thoughts and unhelpful behaviours, causing a vicious circle. Your appearance becomes something you think about all the time, which then affects your mood, leaving you feeling low, frustrated, ashamed or guilty.

When you're feeling insecure your thoughts will tend to take the form of (totally nonsensical) 'facts': 'I am ugly'; 'Everyone notices my ears'; 'My legs are too fat'. These are not facts – they are your biased mind's opinions, guesses and hypotheses. Your preoccupation with your appearance has messed up how your mind processes information, meaning you accept these thoughts as undeniable truths when in fact they're complete and utter twaddle. However, they seem totally reasonable to you at the time so they'll go on to affect your mood, body and behaviour.

Preoccupation is at the core of body image problems as it's near-enough impossible to get a realistic perspective on anything without getting some distance from it, which you can't when you're in the midst of a fixation. We'll teach you how to step back from your thoughts and stop unhelpful behaviours that feed your fixation.

Faulty thought-processing

Why do you think badly about yourself? We discuss thoughts and all their conniving tricks in detail later on in the book (see Chapter 7), but it's important to start recognising what's happening now so you get an idea of what's triggering this negativity.

To manage the volume of information your mind has to process day-to-day your brain chooses what to flag up to your consciousness, cherry-picking what it deems important or note-worthy. When you are preoccupied by something, it is primed to look for all the information on that subject, like a giant spotlight swinging around until it finds what it wants to illuminate.

For example, think back to when you last really wanted something – a new phone, bag or book, for example – and suddenly you see the object of your desire everywhere. Hundreds of those phones, bags or books haven't just miraculously appeared overnight; you're just paying more attention to them.

If you're constantly thinking about your appearance, you've trained your brain to look for information that backs up your negative beliefs. You won't even be consciously aware you're doing it as it's become automatic. The more you act and think as though an aspect of your appearance is a problem, the more your brain looks out for any 'proof' to back up your thoughts, dismissing any evidence that doesn't tally with your preoccupation, for example: 'She only complimented me out of pity, really she thinks I look awful'.

This diagram shows how your thoughts and behaviours combine to aggravate your negative body image:

Start accepting negative thoughts as facts: 'I *am* ugly/ not good enough'

Preoccupied with particular feature

Seek out information to back up this view, dismissing anything that contradicts the belief

Start trying to manage how you look: diets/ make-up/constant mirror-checking etc.

Thoughts like 'I need to change' and behaviours like constant mirror-checking, faddy diets and repetitive make-up reapplication aren't helping – they're actually just feeding your fears.

If you stopped thinking about your supposed 'flaw' and indulging unhelpful behaviours you'd feel more beautiful – it's that simple. Giving yourself some space from your thoughts will give you a far more realistic and healthy perspective of your body.

Theory A and Theory B

There are two theories regarding how you look:

Theory A: You have a physical problem, flaw or defect. You have to engage in behaviours to stop others becoming aware of it.

Theory B: You think you have a physical problem, flaw or defect. It's not a fact, it's an opinion – a belief based upon your own preoccupations. The actions you take to manage this belief actually make you feel worse.

So, Theory B looks pretty reasonable to us. How about you? Yet Theory A is the one you've no doubt adhered to for a long time, even though it makes you feel sad, insecure, miserable and inhibited. Theory A is perpetuating the problem under the guise of 'making things better'. It's complete guff. No matter what you look like, you can be successful in life, have great friends and meaningful relationships. Your only problem is the way you feel and think about your appearance. Physical attractiveness is a tiny part of a massive picture. You are so much more than your appearance. Everyone comes in different shapes and sizes, everyone has different features and yet we all get on with it and tick along together. There is no one-look-fits-all. That's not how the world works (despite what you think). All you have to do now is learn how to appreciate what you've got.

We want you to switch to Theory B – remember that thoughts aren't facts. Just because you think something doesn't make it true. You can change your thoughts to reflect the reality of the situation: that it's not your looks that have to change, it's the way you think about them. The strategies in this book will teach you that you can feel beautiful by simply thinking differently about your appearance and stopping negative behaviours.

⑤ Symptom checklist

Overleaf are some common thoughts, emotions, behaviours and physical symptoms that affect people who are insecure about their looks. Tick off the ones that apply to you. Starting to think about how negative body image affects you personally will show you how your reactions are all related and how they're contributing to that vicious circle shown opposite. This will give you more options for making changes.

Thoughts

- ❑ Comparing yourself: 'I don't look as good as him/her'
- ❑ Self-critical: 'I hate myself for looking this way/I look so ugly'
- ❑ Self-blaming: 'I can't believe I failed that diet/can't fix the way I look'
- ❑ Judgemental: 'No one will ever want to be with me when I look this terrible'
- ❑ Mind-reading: 'He/she is talking about me. They're judging me'
- ❑ Low self-esteem: 'It doesn't matter what I look like as I'm not good enough anyway'
- ❑ Explain away compliments: 'They only said that because they feel sorry for me'
- ❑ Using appearance as a marker of future success/failure: 'Things will be better when I lose weight'
- ❑ Ruminating on the past: 'Why can't I look like I used to?'
- ❑ Indulging worries: 'What if I don't get the job because of how I look?'

Emotions

❑ Shame	❑ Embarrassment	❑ Low self-esteem
❑ Anxiety	❑ Frustration	❑ Jealousy/envy
❑ Low mood	❑ Anger	
❑ Sadness	❑ Guilt	

Behaviour

- ❑ Constantly checking and altering your appearance, e.g. re-applying make-up or changing your hair during the day
- ❑ Comparing your appearance to others, e.g. actively hunting out pictures of celebrities online

❑ Constantly looking at photographs of yourself and analysing your 'flaws'

❑ Looking up diets, contributing to weight-loss forums, reading articles on attractiveness

❑ Frequently weighing or measuring yourself

❑ Choosing clothes that determine how you look that day, e.g. 'fat clothes' versus 'thin clothes'

❑ Constantly checking mirrors or any reflective surfaces

❑ Wearing heavy make-up

❑ Taking up faddy and unsustainable diets

❑ Isolating yourself/becoming withdrawn, e.g. avoiding socialising, staying inside

❑ Defensive body language, e.g. covering your mouth when you smile or covering your face with your hair

❑ Drinking more alcohol or taking drugs (medicinal or recreational)

❑ Changing your eating habits, e.g. restricting or bingeing

❑ Avoiding challenges and new opportunities

❑ Asking others for reassurance about how you look

❑ Avoiding physical intimacy or sex

❑ Investigating cosmetic surgery procedures

Physical symptoms

❑ Tense limbs/hunched shoulders

❑ Tightening in the chest area

❑ Increased heart rate

❑ Change in breathing, such as becoming short of breath

❑ Tired

❑ Sluggish

❑ Low motivation

❑ Poor posture

❑ Distracted

❑ Fidgety

❑ Poor concentration

❑ Nauseous/nervous stomach

Ⓢ Your own mind map

We'd like you to fill in your own mind map. Focus on a recent event that made you feel unhappy with your appearance, using these questions as a guide:

1 **Event:** What happened? What situation triggered this mind map?
2 **Thoughts:** When you were in the situation, what went through your mind (what was your stand-out thought)?
3 **Emotions:** How did you feel emotionally (for example, anxious, low, guilty, resigned, ashamed)?
4 **Physicality:** How did your body react – did you tense up, did your heart race, did you start to sweat?
5 **Behaviour:** What action did you take or think about taking?

Remember, you can start from any point in the mind map. If you remember a sudden flush of embarrassment and anxiety flooding your body (emotions), work backwards from there – what event/physical feeling/behaviour/thought triggered those emotions? We have filled out another sample mind map to help you get started (see opposite).

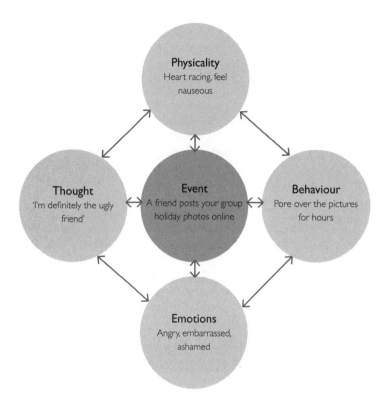

Review: Can you see how the four points all trigger and are triggered by each other, maintaining habitual negative patterns? Analysing one event like this will make you aware of how you deal with body image issues personally. The better you get at identifying your thoughts, behaviours, physicality and emotions, the more options you're giving yourself for making changes.

If you're a very physical person you might find you can tune into what's going on by focusing on your body first, i.e. by realising your stomach is in knots and so using that as your starting point: what caused that feeling? It was when my boss shouted at me. What did I think? 'He wouldn't shout at Anna because she's beautiful'. What did I do? Throw up my lunch with nerves. Pick whichever section strikes a chord with you first and then work from there.

Your thoughts, behaviour and body all act as intervention points – you can change your habitual negative responses to more positive ones, which will then affect your emotions.

⑤ Thoughts aren't facts

+ Write down 'Thoughts aren't facts' somewhere and read it every day. Yes, every single day
+ Next time you catch a thought masquerading as a fact in your head, put 'I think' in front of it and challenge it. For example, 'Everyone's looking at my fat ankles' becomes 'I think everyone's looking at my fat ankles' This key difference will identify the thought as an opinion, not a globally accepted truth
+ Next, challenge it: what proof do you have for this thought? Is everyone really looking at your ankles or are they just going about their daily lives? Are you in fact just projecting your fears and anxieties onto them? Can you pick out three people who aren't looking at them? Of course you can! See? The thought's complete gibberish

Review: This is a key aspect of your new body image regime. When you think, 'I look awful', 'I'll feel happier when I look better' it's very easy to accept these thoughts as facts and feel bad about them. They are just thoughts, not facts. They do not represent reality. Accepting this will be a huge weight off your mind. Starting to pick up on these thoughts will flag up how often you put yourself down with all-encompassing statements that are in fact total nonsense.

Next steps …

Practise filling out a mind map for various situations that have triggered body image anxieties, for example, attending a party, having to make a presentation at work, going on a date or going to the gym. The better you get at identifying your different responses the easier it'll be when you come to change them. By starting to really think about how you personally react to body image you're already questioning your default negative settings and starting to look for a different point of view, which is brilliant. The next chapter is all about challenging negative behaviours that are exacerbating your preoccupation with appearance.

Thoughts to take away

✓ CBT will show you how your thoughts, behaviour, emotions and body are all connected, giving you options for making changes

✓ Filling in mind maps will break situations down, showing you how unrealistic and unfair many of your thoughts are and how unhelpful your resulting actions can be

✓ Thoughts aren't facts: your thoughts are just your brain's negatively skewed opinions. Accepting them as such will make you realise how much you put yourself down. Stop!

3

Stopping Bad Body Image Behaviour

Your behaviour influences your thoughts, mood and body. If you're feeling insecure you're more likely to act in ways you think help, but which actually make you feel worse. This chapter will teach you how to make sure what you're doing is making you feel beautiful.

Why actions really do speak louder than words

How you choose to act in a situation will influence your thoughts, emotions and body. For example, screaming at your boss will make you think, 'This is going to end very badly for me', while your body tenses up and your mood plummets. It's the same with behaviours associated with your appearance. You may think what you're doing is helping you to feel more confident about how you look, but unfortunately a lot of behaviours associated with low body image actually only make you feel worse, feeding your preoccupation with looks and aggravating feelings of self-doubt.

Here is an example to illustrate what we mean:

Reality bites

Nick was on a dinner date with Kath. They'd been out a couple of times before and while he thought it was going well, he wasn't sure how she felt. She'd tried to kiss him during the last date, but he'd dodged it – he was so insecure about his big gappy teeth he felt nervous kissing people. He really liked Kath though, and so had been pleased when she'd agreed to go out with him again.

He left the table, heading to the bathroom for the third time to make sure he still looked OK. He straightened his shirt and checked his teeth in the mirror – his stupid, large, buck teeth. God, he hated them. He looked like a donkey.

Returning to the table, he ordered another bottle of wine, not realising his date had hardly touched her glass. Feeling quite drunk, he became loud, brash and annoying. Kath soon made an excuse and left. Later that night, Nick received a text saying: 'It was lovely meeting you, but we just don't have any chemistry'. Nick felt as if he'd been punched in the stomach. He couldn't believe his teeth had got in the way of him finding a partner yet again.

Nick's behavioural mind map looks like this:

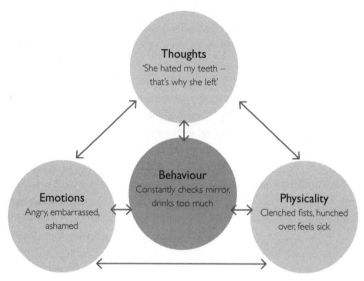

Thoughts
'She hated my teeth —
that's why she left'

Behaviour
Constantly checks mirror,
drinks too much

Emotions
Angry, embarrassed,
ashamed

Physicality
Clenched fists, hunched
over, feels sick

Instead of helping with his insecurity, Nick's behaviour actually caused him more problems. By constantly checking his teeth he was feeding his preoccupation with appearance, which led to him drinking too much in order to feel more confident.

In reality, Nick's date liked his gappy teeth. She thought they made him look fun, approachable and a laugh. She'd actually left because he'd spent half an hour in the bathroom during their two-hour date, which was just plain rude. He'd drunk too much and become a bit of a drag. Also, he'd avoided kissing her, which made her feel insecure. His teeth had nothing to do with it.

Behaviour blues

Your 'safety' behaviours may make you feel better in the short-term (in Nick's case constant mirror-checking and drinking), but it actually only aggravates your insecurity long-term. Nick's fixation with his teeth means he can't get any distance or perspective on the situation. He's convinced his teeth ruined everything when actually his behaviour messed things up.

Take starting a diet, for example. You believe losing weight will make you feel more confident, you feel good for taking action and for sticking to the diet rules (short-term mood lift). Then, if you slip up self-recrimination and negative thinking pile in, for example: 'I failed because I always fail', 'I'm never going to reach my dream weight so am never going to be happy', 'I have no will power'. Most diets fail (see Chapter 5), so the end result is you feel even worse about yourself – not only do you still feel overweight, but a failure too.

From the tick list we asked you to fill out in Chapter 2 (see pages 34–5) you should be becoming more aware of your own behavioural reactions to body image anxieties. You probably never realised it before, but these behaviours will be contributing to your insecurities and low self-esteem. You may think looking in a mirror four times an hour or weighing yourself every day are harmless quirks, but they're not. Behaviours like this change how you view yourself. Not only are you focusing wholly on your supposed 'flaw', but you're seeing yourself as a collection of parts (flawed parts) rather than as a whole: 'My hair looks good today, but my eyes are too tired'; 'If I only eat half this biscuit I won't put any weight on my thighs' or in Nick's case: 'My teeth ruin everything'. Not only this, but some behaviours become routines that dictate your mood and therefore your day, such as a good number on the weighing scales = a good day and good mood; a bad number = a bad day and bad mood; perfect make-up = a good day and good mood while forgetting to bring your concealer to work = a bad day and bad mood.

You might also find yourself withdrawing from life: socialising less, stopping activities you used to enjoy, bingeing on food, watching endless hours of TV, ignoring the phone or doorbell or using alcohol or drugs to numb your feelings. Isolating yourself will fuel your insecurity. Spending time alone gives you more opportunity to dwell on your anxiety and removes the possibility of experiencing good things that would naturally lift your mood. By locking yourself away, you have no chance to disprove the negative theories you hold about yourself.

Your life should not be dictated by habitual negative behaviours. Think of it this way: even the most confident person in the world would start to feel dissatisfied with how they looked if they spent that much time focused on their appearance.

The pros and cons of bad body image behaviour:

Pros	Cons
✦ None Zilch Zero Nada	✦ Aggravates insecurities (the vicious circle – the more you think about your 'flaws', the worse you feel about them) ✦ Your mood can be dictated by these behaviours. For example 'wrong' weight on the scales = bad mood and a bad day ✦ You may withdraw from life, see less of friends and lose crucial social support. By isolating yourself, you have no chance of disproving your negative beliefs by gaining new information (such as by having a great time when you go out) ✦ You may start behaving out of character, e.g. snapping at people or ignoring them ✦ Everything takes longer as you're distracted by thoughts about your appearance. Also, the behaviours themselves take up valuable time ✦ You don't listen to what people say – you're trapped within your own head ✦ You see yourself as a collection of parts, not a whole ✦ You may use alcohol or drugs to mask insecurities ✦ You blame your physical flaw for bad behaviour, such as, 'I only did that because I'm ugly', 'No one cares what I do because I'm ugly' ✦ You believe things will go wrong and therefore behave in ways that ensure they do (your beliefs become self-fulfilling prophecies)

Bad body behaviours stop you doing the things you want to do, narrowing and tainting your experiences. They may even stop you striving to reach goals as not only do they take up valuable time, but they eat away at your confidence in other parts of life: 'They'll give the promotion to the good-looking guy instead of me'; 'If I can't even finish a diet how will I manage a team of people at work?'. In fact, a new government survey found one in five people in the UK have avoided going for a job they wanted because of body image anxiety.

Becoming more aware of these things will flag up how much you make them a reality and give you the option to choose whether you want to continue. Many of these actions will have become habitual, meaning you do them on autopilot. They are such a natural part of your life, you don't even really think about them. You just automatically check your reflection or cover your mouth when you laugh. It's like checking your phone – how often do you pick up your phone without even thinking about it? You probably have no idea, right? Well, once you start paying attention we bet you'd be astonished by how often you look at it without consciously deciding to. That's what this chapter is all about: starting to identify bad behaviours, recognise that they're unhelpful and then reduce the amount of time you carry them out until you can stop altogether, breaking the cycle: feel insecure → unhelpful behaviour → feel worse.

Checked out

'Checking' is one of the most common forms of body image behaviour. While it's natural to peer into a mirror/reflective surface now and then to check you don't have lettuce stuck in your teeth, it becomes problematic when you're looking all the time. If it's getting to a point where checking is holding up your day it's time to make changes. The trouble is, it's become automatic (you don't even realise you're doing it) so you would never consider it 'a problem' (like Nick in the previous example – the fact that he spent a quarter of the date in the bathroom wouldn't have crossed his mind). You have to become aware of it before you can combat it.

Examples of checking:

+ Looking in a mirror or reflective surface (e.g. windows, camera phones reversed to 'selfie' mode)

+ Checking on a specific feature, such as pinching skin, measuring areas of your body with your hands, pulling your skin to measure elasticity, feeling/touching spots

+ Constantly re-applying make-up or checking it's still doing what it's meant to be doing

+ Checking in with others on how you look, for example, asking for reassurance, trying to convince people you look terrible or have a flaw, asking whether this 'flaw' looks okay, worse than normal or whether it's hidden

The ability to be able to check can make you feel relieved in the short-term ('I know my mirror's in my bag so I can check in ten minutes'), but the very fact you have to check again and again and again means it's not achieving anything in the long-term. The actual act itself has become a reassurance – as long as you can check, you'll feel better. If that ability to seek reassurance is taken away (such as losing your mirror, not being near any reflective surfaces, not having anyone around to ask) then you'll start to panic. There is a direct correlation between checking and your mood: if you can check you'll feel okay, if you can't check you'll feel awful. What you're actually checking becomes pretty much irrelevant – you know exactly what you look like because you keep checking! Nothing's going to have changed dramatically in ten minutes or a few hours.

Example: Getting shirty

Nina knew she shouldn't have worn this shirt today. It was too small and made her look fat. Sitting in a meeting with six other people, all she could think about was whether the buttons were noticeably straining over her breasts and stomach. Robbed of the ability to dart to the toilet every half an hour to check her appearance she felt terribly exposed. She kept peering down at herself to try to see how it might look to others, but obviously she didn't have their viewpoint. She then realised she could vaguely see her reflection in the picture on the opposite wall, so shifted around until she could peer at herself.

'Nina, what do you think?' someone suddenly asked. She jumped. Everyone was looking at her. She hadn't heard a word anyone had said for the previous ten minutes.

Nina's mind map
looked like this:

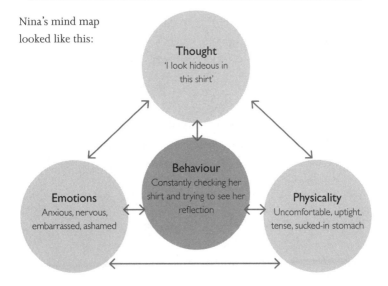

The silly thing is, even if Nina's shirt had been gaping open, that would have been preferable to squirming in her chair, looking distracted and missing the entire meeting. However, it wasn't! One look was enough to confirm that. By constantly checking she was just feeding her fear.

The pros and cons of checking:

Pros	Cons
✦ A tiny short-term relief at your ability to check. A relief that's only present at all because checking is making you feel insecure!	✦ Distracts you from other tasks ✦ Feeds your fear and affects your mood negatively ✦ Means you can't enjoy anything fully as you're always worrying ✦ Upsets/annoys/distracts those close to you ✦ Doesn't work for long and then you have to check again ✦ Clogs up your head with thoughts on your appearance

⑤ Reality check

There are two parts to this strategy.

1 **A** For one whole day we want you to check as much as you can
   – perhaps even more than you would normally. It doesn't matter
   what form that checking takes (for example, asking people for
   reassurance, looking at your reflection, pinching your skin), just do it
   whenever it crosses your mind.

   B Make a tally in your notebook of how many times you check. At the
   end of the day add up the total.

   C Ask yourself: Did the checking make me feel:
   - ✦ More or less certain about how I look?
   - ✦ Better or worse emotionally?
   - ✦ More or less preoccupied with my appearance?

2 **A** The next day only check once. Yes, that's it. Try to be really strict with
   yourself, so ignore the mirror in the bathroom, for example.

However, if you check more than once without thinking, don't berate yourself for it, just be aware of it so that the next time you go to check automatically you'll be able to stop yourself.

B Make a tally of how many times you checked (again, if it's more than once, don't get angry with yourself. As long as the number of times has decreased from the day before you're on the right track).

C Ask yourself: Did checking less make me feel:
   + More or less certain about how I look?
   + Better or worse emotionally?
   + More or less preoccupied with my appearance?

Top tip: Note down any obstacles that might get in the way of limiting the checking and work around them, such as if your compact mirror is always easily accessible, leave it at home. Or, if this feels too scary at first, put it somewhere that's not easily accessible, like in a zipped-up pocket in your bag. The fact you then have to hunt for it will make you more aware of what you're doing, so you snap out of autopilot.

Review: Hopefully checking less made you feel better emotionally. Most people feel incredibly liberated after completing this strategy as they realise that not only can they break free of their checking chains, but they actually feel a whole lot better *not* checking. By becoming more aware of how often you check and what form the checking takes you're taking control of your behaviour and how you feel about it. You're taking positive action and that should feel good. Yes, you're restricting access to something you've relied on for a long time to make yourself feel 'safe', but it's time to change. Checking isn't helping. It isn't reassuring. It doesn't make you feel safe. This strategy should prove that it's making you feel worse. Continue decreasing your checking (don't get angry if you slip up – changing habits takes time) and make this strategy part of your daily routine.

Thoughts
'I didn't realise how often I check or that it made me feel so anxious'

Behaviour
Decrease amount of checking

Emotions
Upbeat, feel more in control

Physicality
Calm, neutral

Mirror, mirror on the wall

Research has shown that negative body image is reinforced by time spent in front of mirrors, but this doesn't mean they should be considered an enemy. The simple tips below will make looking into them less distressing and time-consuming:

+ Stand at a slight distance from the mirror, so you can take in most, if not all, of your body. If it's a pocket mirror, don't pull it right up to an individual feature, but ensure it shows your whole face. You need to start seeing yourself as an entire package rather than a selection of parts

+ Focus on what you see rather than what you feel/think, remaining aware of any thoughts masquerading as facts passing through your mind, such as 'I look awful'. Do you really? Are you being unfair?

⋯∴

+ Don't use magnifying mirrors. These are evil as far as you're concerned.
  We're banning them

+ Leave your compact mirror at home or put it somewhere different, so you
  have to *choose* to look in it rather than doing so automatically

+ Consider rearranging your living space so you aren't constantly running
  into mirrors whenever you turn around

+ Give yourself a time limit in front of the mirror. After you've finished using
  it for something practical, like doing your hair or putting on make-up, walk
  away. Learn to check and then move on, rather than loitering and actively
  searching for problems

+ Don't avoid mirrors altogether! Avoidance is not the answer (it will only
  aggravate your fears, turning your reflection into a bogeyman). This is
  about learning to use mirrors practically – looking at yourself fairly –
  without abusing them. You need to start getting used to your image as
  it really is, without dwelling on imagined 'flaws'. You are not too awful to
  look at!

⑤ Ditch the scales
+ Only weigh yourself once a week or not at all

Like checking, weighing yourself constantly feeds your fixation with
appearance. You end up becoming reliant on a machine to tell you whether
you look acceptable or not. STOP! This is ridiculous. Neither weight nor
your BMI (body mass index) tell you anything substantial about body
composition or health. Everyone's built differently and so weigh different
amounts regardless of what they look like. You may be heavier than
someone else, but much slimmer because of muscle mass or water
retention. You may be classed as obese according to the BMI scale when in

fact you're a sportsperson at the peak of your physical fitness – you just have heavy muscles.

Everyone's weight fluctuates throughout the day by up to 4–6 lb, dependent on what you've digested, body hydration, your menstrual cycle (for women, obviously), bowel/bladder functions – even outside temperature and humidity. There is no such thing as a 'true' weight, only a measure of your weight at one particular moment that's impossible to compare with anyone else's.

As far as how you look physically, weighing yourself is pretty useless. Your eating habits, exercise regime, activity patterns and other self-care choices are much more important. Also, if you're constantly weighing yourself you're setting yourself up for a pass/fail each day, dependent on the results, affecting your mood.

Try to instigate a positive regime around weighing yourself – using the scales as an information tool rather than the harbinger of doom it currently is. If you want to weigh yourself only do it once a week, at the same time, on the same scales, wearing the same clothes (or nothing at all). Measuring your weight weekly will help you to get an accurate impression of your long-term weight trends.

Top tip: If you don't think you can cut down on weighing yourself more than once a week give your scales to someone else to look after for safe-keeping or remove them from their usual place after you've had your weekly weigh-in so you actively have to go and find them. This will stop you sneakily stepping on them if they're easily accessible.

Snapping out of behaviour autopilot

Coming up is a list of other behaviours that may have become habitual and that are feeding your craving for negative body news, with tips on how to stop them.

None of the things listed here will make you feel good about yourself. They may provide short-term relief, but this will turn into long-term angst as you're just perpetuating the myth that you need to change something to feel happy. Simply stopping these behaviours will make you feel happier!

Stop re-applying make-up

You may think an innocent 'top-up' means nothing in the grand scheme of things, but for people with body image anxieties, re-applying make-up aggravates preoccupations with appearance.

✦ Apply it once at the beginning of the day and leave it at that

Wear less make-up

Make-up can become a mask to hide behind. By decreasing the amount you wear you'll feel more in control of your appearance, even if it feels strange at first not looking how you're used to looking. You're being brave by breaking your routine and stepping out of your comfort zone. Doing this will make you realise how other people don't notice small details that mean such a lot to you and if they do notice, they have no idea it's a big deal. While you may feel your face looks totally naked, no one else will raise an eyebrow. By mixing things up you'll realise that your 'mask' doesn't define you.

✦ Cut one thing out of your make-up routine every day (for example, don't use blusher or don't put eyeliner on your bottom lid)

Stop researching your 'flaw' online

If you regularly look up diets, celebrity pictures, surgery, forums that discuss appearance (such as 'thinspiration' websites), or analyse pictures of yourself, you need to start cutting down so you can eventually cut out doing it altogether. This activity is chipping away at your self-esteem and is fuelling your fixation on looks.

✦ For one day tally up how much time you spend online researching stories, forums, pictures or surgeries concerned with appearance. The next day cut down that time by 10 per cent, then another 10 per cent the next, until you can go a whole day without looking anything up

Top tip: Log out of any 'appearance-focused' websites you've signed up to and close down any pages you've bookmarked so they're not so easily accessible. By actively having to log in you'll snap out of autopilot and have to choose whether to continue or not.

Tell people what you're doing

Social support can be an incredible motivator when making a change like this. Too often we get caught up in our own thoughts, worries and fears and sharing them with someone else can relieve the pressure and give you a new perspective.

✦ Consider informing your closest friends or your partner that you're trying to stop doing some of these things, so they can support you and know what to look out for

Stop seeking reassurance

We all love a compliment, but constantly asking others about your looks will only make you question yourself. Enjoy the compliments you're given without having to ask for them.

✦ If you're constantly asking for reassurance (such as, 'Does this top hide my arms?', 'I look so grim today') tell people if you ask again they should ignore you. You don't need to make a big deal of it, just say, 'Sorry, I know that's really annoying – just ignore me next time!'

✦ Now you've started noticing you're asking, hopefully you'll be able to stop yourself the next time you go to do it automatically

Don't withdraw from socialising

Don't let fears about your appearance dictate your life. As mentioned on the previous page social support is a key factor in feeling happy. Staying at home will breed insecurity as you're alone with your thoughts.

You don't have to talk about your body image with your friends, just have a laugh and enjoy their company (laughing is proven to boost your mood). Every time your thoughts drift back to appearance, acknowledge them without getting into them or getting angry at yourself, and simply bring your mind back to the present moment. It's all too easy to spend every day stuck in your own head, so you don't enjoy life fully because you're not present.

+ Say yes to social events. See your friends. Have a laugh. Organise something yourself
+ While you're working through this book try to hang out with people with a healthy body image and healthy relationship to food. Avoid those who aggravate your own insecurities – people with eating disorders, who exercise excessively and people who seek reassurance constantly
+ For the time being avoid people who make you feel worse about how you look – you know who they are

Stop being self-deprecating or indulging in 'fat talk'

Constantly putting yourself down and indulging in 'fat talk', no matter how jokily you do it, will only make you feel worse (as proven by numerous studies).

+ If someone compliments you just say, 'thanks'; don't respond by putting yourself down or dismissing it
+ Don't bring weight into any compliments you give. Say, 'Those trousers are lovely', not 'Those trousers are slimming'
+ Don't 'excuse' other people's looks or weight for them (such as, 'You're only a Large because you have big boobs') and if someone does it to you,

brush it off as a mark of their own insecurity, not a reflection on you

✦ Stop discussing what you're allowed or not allowed to eat according to some rule in your head (for example, 'I shouldn't have a slice of cake'). You're not only making yourself feel bad, you're making others feel bad. If you don't want some, just say, 'No thanks'

✦ Stop posting thoughts online about exercise, weight or food. By writing these things down you're giving them undue attention and you're aggravating your preoccupations by waiting for responses from others

✦ Don't say 'fat' or 'thin' at all. Banish them from your vocabulary

Stop 'appearance-altering' beauty treatments

Breaking 'beauty routines' will take you out of your comfort zone, which (if you hadn't noticed) we're pretty keen on at this stage. We're not talking about massages or manicures; we're talking about the treatments that promise you'll look different at the end. By cancelling those, you'll hopefully realise that you don't need them, that life carries on just fine and that you can feel great without them. (You'll also save yourself some money, which is a bonus.) You can always go back to the treatments when you've finished the book, but hopefully by then you won't feel they're essential to your self-esteem, rather they're just occasional treats.

✦ While working through this book, cancel all beauty treatments such as facial peels, fat-loss wraps or eyelash extensions

Cancel or postpone all cosmetic surgical procedures

Surgery is a big deal and if you're reading this book that's a good indication that you believe you can feel better about how you look without going under the knife. Please give this process a go before committing to surgery, just until you're sure you've explored all avenues.

✦ Please cancel any cosmetic surgical procedures you have booked in – just for the time being. If you get to the end of the book and feel you'd still like to proceed and are confident you know what to expect, both physically and emotionally, go for it

Don't wear 'fat' or 'thin' clothes

If you have 'fat' and 'thin' clothes, picking which ones to wear can dictate your mood and therefore your day, such as 'I've failed because I'm in my "fat" jeans today'.

✦ Stick to a wardrobe that has no body image connotations

Stop dieting

The way we all regularly go on about dieting is a complete farce. The only way to stop food becoming an all-encompassing obsession is to stick to a healthy and realistic eating plan. Luckily we've detailed one for you in Chapters 5 and 6.

✦ This is a big one. Whatever diet you are on right now, STOP

Exercise

Exercise will make you feel better emotionally and physically.

✦ See Chapter 9 for our recommendations on introducing exercise into your life in a totally non-intimidating way

Thoughts to take away

✓ Body image behaviours feed your preoccupation with appearance, making you feel insecure. Stop them and you'll feel stronger, happier and more confident

✓ Stepping out of your comfort zone will make you realise it's not your appearance that's holding you back, it's how you feel about your appearance and you're on the right track to feeling differently!

✓ You don't need to 'check', weigh yourself, hide away or dress certain ways. Try doing things differently for a bit. You'll be amazed at how brave you can be and how good you'll feel

4

The Emotion Picture

Your emotions colour everything you do. If you feel insecure, you'll behave in ways that perpetuate your negative body image beliefs – so you end up feeling worse. In this chapter you'll learn how to manage your emotions, to start feeling more self-assured and confident.

In the mood

Your emotions act as guides to understanding what's happening in your life so you can process experiences and move forward. They shape your beliefs and the meaning you give things. As much as we'd like to feel air-punchingly brilliant all the time, it's just not realistic. We were born able to feel the full spectrum of emotions – from euphoria to despair – and you slide up and down this scale depending on what's going on.

It's human nature not to want to feel bad, so we have a tendency to run away from distress and switch our focus to other things – often our bodies (ironically with much the same result: distress). Bodies are a handy scapegoat for when life feels out of control (for example, 'This situation would be better if only I could get rid of my spots'). However that isn't to say body image anxieties are only ever symptoms of a separate problem; often they are the problem – you think there's something wrong with your appearance and wish it were different (see Theory A, pages 32–3).

Your mood affects your body image, just as your body image affects your mood – it's bi-directional. For example, when you feel low you're more likely to dislike the way you look, just as if you dislike the way you look you're more likely to feel low. This negative tug-of-war can taint everything, taking your mind off more important things: friends, family, work, life, love, aspirations or the present moment.

Poor body image has been linked to low self-esteem, anxiety, depression and feelings of shame. These emotions will affect your physicality, thoughts and behaviour. Your physical reactions to events are often the most obvious clues to your emotional state of mind, for example, when you're happy you smile and when you're sad you cry. Those are obvious 'non-verbal cues', but your body changes in thousands of subtle ways to reflect how you feel. Your thoughts play their part, too, triggering an emotion or being triggered by one, such as feeling sad might prompt the thought, 'I'm so ugly', just as thinking 'I'm so ugly' will trigger sadness.

Remember: feelings pass. They aren't permanent. No matter how bad you feel, you can and will feel better. Emotions aren't good or bad, they are psychological responses to events. There's nothing wrong with negative emotions: they feel bad, but they're meant to. They're nature's way of telling you there's a problem. The trick is not to aggravate the feelings by doing things to make yourself feel worse. Becoming aware of your emotional responses to thoughts and events will make you feel more in control as you can choose how you want to act in response, rather than blundering along on autopilot, getting stuck in damaging cycles ('Here we go again'/'Why do I always feel like this?'). Feeling more in control will give you a more realistic perspective on things – including your appearance. And, being more realistic will make you feel more beautiful because you won't be obsessing over so-called 'flaws'. You might even come to like the way you look (seriously).

⑤ Learning to identify your emotions

Use the table on the next page to track your emotions for one day. Write down what happened, your feelings, thoughts, behaviour and physical reaction whenever you feel a strong emotional response to an event.

Isolating your responses to a situation breaks down the problem. Rather than just being swamped by an overwhelming feeling, you can start to see the component parts – the domino effect that's perpetuating your body image anxieties. Everything will feel less overwhelming as you're stepping back and getting perspective.

If you find it hard to identify the emotion straight away work through the other sections first and fill in the gaps. Your physical response is usually the most obvious, so often that's the easiest place to start. Also, identifying the original trigger – the event – is crucial. Negative reactions can snowball and it's easy to lose focus on what you're actually feeling anxious or low about.

Situation	Thoughts	Emotions	Physicality	Behaviour
My boss undermined me in front of all my colleagues	'He's so much nicer to good-looking staff'	Embarrassment, anxiety, anger	Tense up, blush, sweaty palms	Eat a box of chocolates
I'm wearing the same dress as someone else at a wedding	'Everyone is thinking how much better she looks in the dress than me'	Shock, hurt, humiliation	Heart racing, short of breath, stomach ache	Keep cardigan on, even though it's 30°C, hide away, spend whole day thinking about it
My friend constantly talks about his exercise regime and how fat he is – even though I'm much bigger	'If he thinks he's fat, he must think I'm a whale'	Frustration, shame, guilt	Hunched shoulders, try to 'get smaller' by curling in on yourself, grit teeth	Wear baggy dark clothes whenever he's around, start avoiding him, eat more when he's there as an act of rebellion

Review: How did you find this exercise – hard, stupid, interesting, enlightening? If you thought it was stupid, why? Is it because you're still a devotee of Theory A (see pages 32–3): that you do actually have a physical problem so trying to feel differently about it is ludicrous? Thinking that way is understandable. You've believed it for a long time so you can't change overnight. However, filling in this table will give you an insight into how you respond to things and how those responses affect each other. Often we're not even aware of how we're feeling when we do things, getting caught up in a whirlwind of emotion and falling back into habits that make us feel 'safe' such as comfort eating, hiding away or wearing nondescript clothes. These behaviours make you feel worse, not better. Learning to identify those patterns will give you intervention points so you can interrupt the cycles and focus on what's actually going on, such as feeling undervalued by your boss.

Shame

Shame can be a real problem for people experiencing body image issues. There are two types: external and internal.

External shame: The belief that others don't think you're up to scratch

Internal shame: When you don't meet your own exacting standards

There is a difference between guilt and shame. Guilt is 'a feeling of having committed a known wrong', whereas shame, according to social work professor Brené Brown, is an intensely painful feeling associated with believing you are intrinsically flawed, therefore unworthy of love. For example, you may feel guilty eating a piece of cake. This act breaks an internal rule and you feel guilty because you know you didn't have to eat it. However, shame suggests you have no choice – that you are irrevocably damaged/defective.

Research into the effect these two emotions have on making positive changes has found that guilt can be motivational – people see they have options and want to make changes. However, shame can actually increase unhelpful behaviours as sufferers believe they're hopeless. One study found that participants exposed to 'fat-shaming' messages were more likely to consume high-calorie snacks.

These findings are relevant to all body image anxieties, not just weight. Recognising shame is fundamental to learning how to feel more beautiful because you can challenge it: 'Have I succeeded at things I've tried in the past?'; 'Do I have talents to be proud of?' Everyone is insecure about something and, yes, you will have succeeded at things (which you probably later dismissed as unimportant). Trying something that frightens you is courageous; something to be proud of. It doesn't matter how big or small. Don't undervalue what you have to give and what other people see in you. The strategies in Chapter 8 will push you in the right direction to finding self-appreciation.

Once more with feeling

The table you filled out on page 64 could look totally different. Tuning into your emotions, curbing bad behaviour and learning to challenge negative thoughts (Chapter 7 onwards) will give you a far more realistic, happier perspective on events. At the moment you are not being realistic, no matter how much you think you are. Your emotions, thoughts, physicality and behaviour have convinced you your appearance is holding you back, when in reality they are the things holding you back. They're pretty convincing swines, we'll give them that, but it's time to stand up for yourself.

By recognising knee-jerk emotional reactions you'll be stepping back from them and giving yourself space to assess what you want to do instead of indulging old insecurities. When you next feel low or anxious, rather than scoffing a packet of biscuits, snapping at colleagues or spending 20 minutes analysing the size of your bum, you'll be able to view things calmly: what's really making me feel angry/humiliated/guilty? Does my boss undermine everyone, not just me? Is my appearance really hurting my relationship or is my partner actually a horrible prat? Will I really only get a promotion if I lose weight – don't I have all the skills I need right now?

Taking these steps will change your interpretations of an event – the basis of your negative body image. At the moment your interpretations are wrong, stupid, unfair and outdated. It's time to get some new ones.

Ⓢ Reflection time

+ Schedule 15 minutes each day to sit down alone and reflect on what's happened. Write down any worries, insecurities or stressful situations (using the table format on page 64 from the first strategy, if you want) and then label the emotions that accompanied them
+ Every time a worry pops into your head during the day, tell yourself, 'I'll deal with that during my reflection time,' and move on to think about something else

Review: Labelling emotions is a simple way of facing up to them: how did I really feel? Guilty. About what? Failing my diet. Really? Well, I also feel guilty about hating my job. Working out what's actually going on will make you feel more in control. Facing how you feel is frightening, but honestly, once you get into the habit of doing it, it's a relief. Running away from 'bad' emotions only makes them grow. If you can say, 'I feel embarrassed, but I know the feeling is normal and will pass', the emotion loses its power to hurt.

Problem-solving

Many body image anxieties are triggered by stress. Stress is a whole different kettle of fish, however we think it's handy to include a problem-solving strategy here to use whenever you feel life might be getting on top of you and aggravating your body insecurities.

Avoiding stressful situations only makes them worse. We tend to cope better with things once we know what we're dealing with, even if the situation is quite bad. For example, knowing your friend has called the fire brigade when you're stuck up a tree. You're still stuck up there, but at least you know there's a plan in place. When you're faced with something hard and the outcome is a mystery you not only feel stressed but will also generate worst-case scenarios ('I'm going to be stuck up here forever') so the best way to limit anxiety is to plan and take action. The following step-by-step guide (with an example under each stage) will make any problem feel more manageable. Feeling more in control of non-appearance-related issues will make you feel more positive about your body image because you're not dwelling, worrying or freaking out about everything.

⑤ Turning mountains into molehills

✦ During your 15 minutes' 'reflection time' (see the strategy on page 66), identify on-going problems or those you're putting off dealing with

✦ Ask yourself 'Can I do anything about it?' If the answer is no (such as 'What if it rains the day of my party?'), STOP worrying about it as you're just wasting time – these things are out of your control. If the answer is yes, follow the steps below

1 Write down clearly what's bothering you.

   I haven't been paid for five weeks and can't afford my rent

2 Brainstorm as many solutions as you can in five minutes, even if the ideas are absurd.

   a *Refuse to go into work*

   b *Go to the payroll office myself*

   c *Send payroll another email*

   d *Threaten to contact lawyers*

   e *Keep phoning payroll until I have an answer*

   f *Ask parents for a loan*

3 Evaluate the pros and cons of each idea. We've used solution c as an example, but you'll need to do this for each idea.

   Pros: *I won't shout at them over email/I'll have a record of all my correspondence*

   Cons: *They won't answer/I've already emailed five times/emails can be ignored*

4 Choose the solution that answers your biggest concerns. There's often more than one way to solve a problem, but start with the one you feel most comfortable with. If it doesn't work, move on to the next. The main thing is you're being proactive.

   Choose solution e with f as a back-up

5 Break down this solution into smaller, achievable steps. What, when and how will you do this? Being detailed means you're more likely to actually start than put it off. Note down anyone else who needs to be

involved. If there's a stage of the plan that's causing problems, work around it – even if it means talking to someone else (admitting to people you need help can be terrifying, but you'll feel so much better). *Go into work early to make the call. Take down the name of whoever I speak to. If no one answers, leave message. Tell boss what's happening so s/he knows why I'm on the phone and stressed. Call again during tea break. If still no luck, ask boss for help. Once I know when I'm getting paid, speak to parents about loan*

6 Do it. Once you've actually put the plan into action you'll feel more motivated to see it through.

7 Evaluate how it went. If nothing was sorted out, go back to your brainstorm and try something else, starting the process again with what you know now as a jumping-off point (such as 'James in payroll is an idiot so I need to speak to someone else'). Whatever happened, give yourself some credit for having a go and facing the situation.

Review: Even if nothing comes of your ideas, just thinking about trying to sort stuff out rather than avoiding doing so will make you feel calmer. Don't get despondent if your ideas don't work. Instead use what you've learned to make a new plan. Facing problems is tough and you should be proud of yourself for taking action. Feeling more in control of non-body-image-related troubles will make you feel stronger in dealing with those that are concerned with appearance.

Body language

We all exhibit non-verbal cues and respond to them in other people. We 'read' mood, personality and character through expressions, tics, posture, stance and behaviour. If someone is standing in an 'open' stance with their shoulders back, chin up and arms relaxed they'll look confident and approachable, whereas if someone has their shoulders hunched, their arms crossed and is looking at the floor they'll look defensive and unapproachable.

By simply exhibiting more positive body language you'll feel more confident. A study published in the *European Journal of Social Psychology* found that people who sat up straight in their chairs were more confident about things they were then asked to write down. They also discovered that posture builds a sense of strength and confidence in social situations too.

If you project an aura of self-assurance (even if you're faking it) people will respond to it, making you feel more self-assured (so you don't have to fake it any more). If you look the part, you'll feel and act the part too. It's such a simple trick for feeling better about your body image.

Ⓢ Keeping up appearances

+ When you notice your shoulders hunched up to your ears, drop them
+ Keep your chin up and head raised
+ Straighten your back, even when you're sitting down
+ Stop using 'body barriers': uncross your arms, stop holding your bag in front of your body, move your fringe out of your eyes and don't cover your mouth when you laugh
+ Make eye contact when you talk to people
+ Dress to impress (yourself). One day next week wear something different – something you wouldn't normally feel brave enough to wear. If you usually only wear dark colours, put on a bright t-shirt or necklace. If you normally wear jeans, put on a skirt. If you normally wear a sombre suit, brighten it up with a colourful tie. Taking risks with your clothes will make you feel courageous
+ Smile. Smiling is actually proven to make you feel happier. Smiles are also contagious – people will smile at you in return, lifting your mood
+ Look out for non-verbal cues in other people. If Becky from next door never meets your eye maybe it's because she's shy rather than rude

Review: While these changes may be a big deal to you, other people will have no idea they're unusual or scary. They're not going to stand on a chair and announce to the office, 'Lizzie's wearing heels for the first time in 12 years – everyone look at them!' They're just going to say, 'Nice heels' and you'll feel great. They will respond to your newly confident appearance positively, which will make you feel more confident. It's a win-win situation.

Next steps ...

You may have noticed we haven't dealt with food yet – food, glorious food. People with body image anxieties often have complicated relationships with eating, food and diet, which is why we've dedicated two chapters to the topic (Chapters 5 and 6). If you don't believe you have any issues surrounding food we'd still recommend you read them as we think you'll find it (hopefully) interesting and useful.

Thoughts to take away

✓ Your emotions don't have to define you or dictate your day. Learning to identify what triggers certain moods will make you feel more in control

✓ Emotions pass; they're not permanent. No matter how low you feel, you can and will feel better

✓ Projecting an aura of confidence through your body language will make you feel more confident and therefore more beautiful

5

Food for Thought

How and why does food play such a big role in body image? This chapter sets out strategies for understanding, acknowledging and challenging your food and diet beliefs.

Why does food play such a big role in body image?

The answer to this question concerns control and change: you control your food intake so it's an easy thing to take the brunt of your emotional insecurity – and eating too much/too little will change your body. While you can't change your nose, scars, hips or height you can change your weight. This knowledge can be seductive when you're feeling insecure.

You have to eat to survive, but other than that it's up to you – what, how, when and whether you eat comes down to personal choice. The choices you make are determined by several different factors:

+ **Your childhood:** The food habits, beliefs and routines you grew up with
+ **Media:** What you read/watch and choose to believe about diets and body shape via information that comes to you from the media
+ **Environment:** What food is available to you according to location or cost
+ **Culture/religion:** What beliefs you live by concerning food and diet
+ **Emotions:** Whether you increase or decrease your food intake dependent on emotions
+ **Social group:** What your friends, peers, family eat or expect you to eat
+ **Health:** How you feel physically when you've eaten certain things or whether you need to lose or gain weight for medical reasons

Dissatisfaction with appearance is a major cause of dieting and issues surrounding food, for example, you think being slimmer will make you happier or more 'acceptable' to others. Or, you think you're too short, but because you can't do anything about that you focus on weight instead ('At least I can be slimmer'). Research shows that poor body image increases the risk of extreme weight- and body-control behaviours.

Messing about with food – whatever form it takes – is a classic case of behavioural short-term gain, but long-term pain (the likes of which we mentioned in Chapter 3). You may feel good initially for taking action and sticking to your diet, but long-term you're aggravating your preoccupation with appearance and feeding your anxieties. Also, by setting yourself food 'rules' you're setting yourself up for a fall because the rules are likely to be unsustainable or unrealistic. Then, when you inevitably do 'fail' or slip up, this sets the tone for your whole day/week/year and initiates a cycle of self-recrimination:

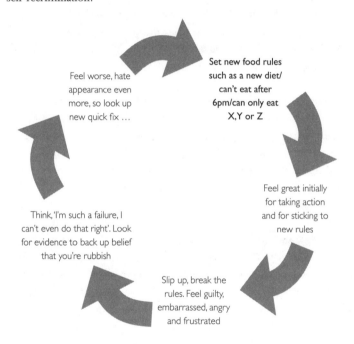

Feel worse, hate appearance even more, so look up new quick fix …

Set new food rules such as a new diet/ can't eat after 6pm/can only eat X,Y or Z

Feel great initially for taking action and for sticking to new rules

Think, 'I'm such a failure, I can't even do that right'. Look for evidence to back up belief that you're rubbish

Slip up, break the rules. Feel guilty, embarrassed, angry and frustrated

It's important not to let food become part of the problem. If you're doing any of the following, it's time to change your mind-set:
+ Thinking about food all the time
+ Constantly dieting

+ Only exercising to work off what you've eaten
+ Eating more or less than 'normal', depending on mood
+ Eating secretly
+ Setting yourself unrealistic or unobtainable weight goals

This chapter is all about recognising what's going on so that you can identify and stop negative patterns, while the next chapter sets out a new healthy eating plan so that food doesn't rule your life and you can learn to enjoy eating again. Food isn't your enemy!

The things that shape how we think about food

Recognising yourself in any of the following explanations should come as a relief. What you're experiencing is really common – you're not alone. You can change your reactions to all of these habits, emotions and thoughts; acknowledging them is the first step in making changes.

Habits learned from childhood

Your family's cultural beliefs, traditions and attitudes to food will have affected how and what you ate growing up, which will have shaped how you view food now. Things such as your parents not letting you leave the table until your plate was clean stick in your mind and grow roots. What you ate growing up will contribute too – whether or not you learnt to cook or ate a balanced diet and if a member of the family had an eating disorder that affects how you view food in relation to appearance now.

Your beliefs surrounding physical beauty

Body shape plays a big part in body image. If you believe you should be heavier or slimmer according to your own personal standard of physical beauty you'll inevitably start trying to control how much and what you eat.

Your environment

Unless you're totally self-sufficient, then food costs money. What you can afford will affect what you choose to eat. Also, much depends on what's available: if there's a fast-food outlet next to your office while the nearest supermarket's three miles away, chances are you'll be munching chips most lunchtimes. There are ways around these obstacles if you look for them, such as investigating cheap, healthy recipes and then bringing food into work or organising a car-share to the supermarket.

Your health

If you are allergic to some foods or react badly to them, this obviously affects what you can eat. However, this only becomes a body image issue when you extend the restrictions unnecessarily, making food and diet the focus of all your attention rather than just some. Health concerns can also affect body image when a natural desire to be a healthy weight spirals into a preoccupation with size.

Using food as a means of communication

Believing certain foods communicate something about you, such as ordering a salad because you think people will expect you to or not eating a chocolate bar because you think people will judge you.

All of these things can lead to the twin terrors of body image: emotional eating and dieting.

Emotional eating

Under- or over-eating can be triggered by your mood. Stress, sadness, jealousy, shame, guilt, boredom, laziness, loneliness and anxiety can all make you reach for the pastries. Even happiness can influence eating patterns, for example, over-eating as a form of 'nesting' when feeling content in a new relationship or as a way to celebrate or reward yourself.

Your upbringing will influence the emotions you attribute to food: food as love, comfort, a treat, distraction or reward versus withholding food as a punishment or using it as a means to make you feel guilty, greedy or ashamed.

Some foods even have a chemical reaction, physically provoking emotions. For example, chocolate is proven to release feel-good chemicals in your brain so you do actually feel better after eating it.

All of these things can prompt us to eat when we feel certain emotions, regardless of whether we're hungry or not, using food to comfort or forget, to soothe or distract.

Good mood = good food

A recent study by University of Delaware associate professor Meryl Gardner found that being in a good mood means you're much more likely to eat healthily. An upbeat mind-set leads to thinking about the future, so you're more interested in feeling good, energised and healthy, whereas a bad mood means you're more likely to choose indulgent food for a short-term lift.

If you have body image anxieties you need to learn how to recognise emotional eating and curb it. Using food as a temporary distraction from a bigger issue will only throw more emotions into the mix, such as adding guilt on top of the grief you feel over your relationship break-up. You're making both food and appearance your focus when neither should be. And physically, by over- or under-eating you're messing with your metabolism (see pages 83–4). If you never deal with the root causes of your distress no amount of dieting or food controls will make you feel better.

⑤ Your emotional food diary

Fill out the following table for one week, monitoring when and what you eat and what mood you're in when you eat it. (Do this over the course of a week so you can't pick a day that doesn't represent a normal routine and/ or deliberately try not to eat emotionally!)

Ignore any reticence you feel about monitoring your food. Yes, it can be weird noting down every little thing you eat, but research shows that people who use food logs have the most positive outcomes when it comes to improving their relationship with food. We'll be asking you to keep several logs throughout this process as a means to making you aware of your own reactions to food and your eating triggers. By recording your habitual behaviour it's easier to see harmful patterns and stop them. Yes, you'll be thinking a lot about food during this process – possibly more than normal – but that's only temporary. As soon as you feel comfortable with your new eating plan you won't need to monitor your food any more and will find you think about it a lot less.

Day	Food consumed (including time)	Mood at time of eating
Monday	8.30am: Blueberry breakfast muffin	Calm
	11am: Shortbread biscuit snack	Bored
	1pm: Cheese and ham baguette	Flustered

Review: Becoming more aware of the moods that accompany your eating will mean that the next time you're stressed/lonely/bored/annoyed/angry and find yourself munching some stale crisps you found in your desk drawer you'll realise what you're doing and snap out of autopilot. You can then ask yourself, 'Do I really want to eat that? Am I hungry? Will eating it make me feel better or worse?' and then choose what to do consciously rather than robotically. It's also worth thinking about the situations that affect you most – feeling unappreciated, having an argument, being ignored, having too much to do – so you'll be more aware of your responses.

Remember: you may feel some relief when you're eating, but it's not actually the food that's making you feel better in that moment – it's you. You've projected a feeling of relief onto the food, but you could easily transfer that association to something else: reading a page in your book, making a coffee, calling a friend, sniffing a favourite perfume or going for a walk.

Why diets are rubbish

Guess what? Diets don't work. Sorry for spitting on your chips, but it's scientifically proven. As a long-term means of losing weight and then maintaining weight loss they don't work. Yes, you might be able to lose 5lb in a week on a stewed cabbage diet, but as soon as you go back to normal food you'll put it back on. Mentally and physically, we're not cut out for diets, but that doesn't stop fad after fad promising you 'your dream body'. We're told that painful and complicated aspects of life can be resolved by changing our appearance. Moreover, we're told that the process is straightforward and unambiguous: 'Follow this diet for a better life!' If you're not cutting out carbs, you're banning sugar or dairy, munching according to blood type or eating like a cave man. The diet industry is big business because when the latest fad inevitably fails you end up starting another one. And another.

If you have a generally healthy body image and genuinely want a quick fix, for example you want to lose weight for a specific event, then do set yourself a diet goal and go for it. Just be prepared to put the weight back on, and then some, when you relax your eating habits again.

A study by University of California, published in the *American Psychologist* journal, followed people on diets for between two and five years. At the end of the programme 83 per cent of participants had either returned to their starting weight or weighed more than before they started. Another study compared changes in weight, eating behaviour, attitudes to food and self-esteem, depression and body image between two groups of women. The first group had to monitor their weight and restrict their calories/fat intake. The second group used a Health At Every Size (HAES) approach, focusing on body acceptance, stopping restrictive eating, becoming aware of internal hunger cues, paying attention to nutritional information and overcoming fears or obstacles to exercise. The results were staggering. At the two-year follow-up, the HAES group showed sustained, significant improvements in total cholesterol, blood pressure, exercise participation and enjoyment, susceptibility to hunger, restricted eating, body dissatisfaction and self-esteem. Meanwhile, the first 'diet' group showed no positive results in any of these areas and reported significantly lower self-esteem, with 53 per cent of the group expressing feelings of failure, compared to 0 per cent of the HAES group.

It's proven: healthy body image translates into healthy bodies and vice versa. If you feel good about yourself, you'll want to look after your body, just as if you look after your body you'll feel good about yourself. By changing your lifestyle (with our healthy eating plan), you'll change your relationship to food, enabling you to stay at a weight that's right for you and stop food obsessions. By feeling healthy rather than sluggish, bloated or starving, you'll find a new appreciation of your body that will engender self-acceptance, making you feel beautiful (yes, really).

Ⓢ Your dieting history

Note down the answers to the following questions:

1 Are you on a diet right now (even though we recommended you stop it immediately!)?
2 How many diets have you started in the last one/two/three years?
3 How often do you reach your target? How do you feel when you do/don't?

4 Do you usually put weight back on when you relax or stop the diet? How does this make you feel?

5 When do you tend to diet: summer/winter/for an event/all the time?

6 When were you last at the weight you wanted to be? Were you genuinely happy at this weight? Did trying to maintain the weight take up a lot of time/energy/headspace?

7 Why did you stop the diets you were on? For example, 'I'd reached my ideal weight/It was unsustainable/Messed with my lifestyle/I was always thinking about food/I got bored'

8 Did the diet(s) work as it/they promised?

9 Does a bad result on the scales or a slip-up on a diet (such as eating a 'banned' food) make you feel bad, guilty, ashamed, annoyed?

Review: Answering these questions should make you more aware of your relationship with dieting – how it makes you feel emotionally and how it affects your body image. Starting to question your beliefs around food, diets and your body is a crucial step in breaking down negative thought and behaviour patterns.

Why diets are a recipe for disaster (ho ho)

Psychologically: Because they aggravate your fixation on body image and perpetuate the self-guilt/shame body image spiral. If you lose weight you see it as a 'success' and store up all the compliments you receive. You may change your body shape short-term, but studies show that it's very rare to maintain this long-term. If you do slip up or 'fail' according to the rules you've set yourself it affects your mood, triggering deeper feelings of self-doubt, which will make you engage in more unhelpful behaviours. Hello vicious circle! You might then dwell on the compliments you received when it was going well, turning them into negatives: 'They said I looked good then, so now I've put on weight I must look bad'.

Biologically: We have to eat to survive. Our body sends us signals alerting us to when it needs feeding, how it feels eating certain things and when to stop eating. If you're constantly chopping and changing your diet or eating irregularly you're interfering with your body's natural processes, which will have dramatic consequences.

Without getting too bogged down in the science, here is a brief explanation of how your body deals with food/hunger/appetite:

Hunger: A sensation in your body that makes you want to eat. It's monitored by a region in your brain called the hypothalamus, which detects your blood-sugar level, how empty your stomach and intestines are and certain hormone levels in your body.

Fullness: Also referred to as 'satiety', it's a feeling of satisfaction triggered by nerves in your gut sending signals to your brain. Increased blood-sugar, feedback from the hypothalamus, and presence of food in the stomach and intestines all make you feel full.

Appetite: A desire for, or interest in, food, caused by sight, smell or thought. Appetite can override hunger and fullness, which is why you may continue eating even after you feel full. You can also have no appetite for food even though you're hungry, for example when you're stressed.

Diets mess with the body's natural regulatory system, affecting your metabolism.

Metabolism: This is the process in which your body extracts the energy it needs from food and is the name for chemical reactions that convert food into fuel. After you eat, enzymes break proteins into amino acids, fats into fatty acids and carbohydrates into simple sugars (such as glucose). Sugar, amino acids and fatty acids can all be used as energy sources by the body when needed. We tend to use calories or kilocalories to measure how much energy there is in food and drink. It's estimated that men require around 2,500 kcals a day and women around 2,000. How much you need depends on height, weight, activity levels, lifestyle and metabolic rate.

When you start eating less than normal, your metabolism slows down. It's not used to surviving on what you're giving it, so it compensates for the energy deficiency by releasing carbohydrates back into the blood, making you feel hungrier. Your blood-sugar levels drop, also contributing to feelings of increased hunger. Your body is shouting, 'Give me what I'm used to!' By slowing down, your metabolism is preserving energy and storing fat. This means as a weight-loss device food restriction doesn't work. You may lose a lot in the first week or so, but research shows that large initial weight loss is from body fluids, not fat, so the loss eventually stalls as your body tries to protect itself.

Faddy diets try to exploit your body's starvation mode by tricking it into believing it's full when it's not (such as by only eating fatty foods or carbs) or by messing with its processes by only eating proteins. The result? You're so hungry and exhausted you give up the diet or 'slip up' and eat the food your body actually needs. It's so excited to receive the food it wants it clings onto it for dear life – storing excess energy as fat while it tries to make up for what it's lost. This is why often you'll put on more weight than you originally lost after giving up a diet. Your metabolism also can't cope if you eat too much. It reaches its optimum level of activity and that's it – it can't do any more. All the excess food is then also stored as fat.

The bottom line: eat what's right for you (not too much or too little) and your metabolism will merrily do what it's meant to do. If you listen to your body by eating when you're hungry and stopping when you're full, you won't shock your metabolism into slowing down. Your body tells you when and what it needs. Listen to your body and you'll feel healthier, more energetic and happier. Simple (see the healthy eating plan in the next chapter).

Anorexia nervosa, Bulimia and EDNOS

Anorexia nervosa: An illness in which you keep your body weight low by dieting, vomiting or exercising excessively (or all of the above). It's caused by a fear of being fat, a desire to be thin and/or a need for control in general.

Symptoms include:

+ Refusing to keep your body weight at or above a minimally normal weight for your age and height
+ Taking drastic measures to control your food intake, such as not eating enough or bingeing, followed by purging via vomiting, use of laxatives, enemas/diuretics
+ Exercising too much
+ Being afraid of putting on weight or becoming fat, even if you are underweight
+ Believing that you are overweight despite the fact that you're not; feeling that your body shape is inextricably linked with who you are; denying the seriousness of your low body weight
+ Missing three or more menstrual cycles in a row
+ Believing that weight-loss is inextricably linked with your personal achievement, confidence and self-esteem

Bulimia: A cycle of eating large quantities of food (bingeing) and then vomiting, taking laxatives, diuretics or using enemas (purging) coupled with exercising or fasting.

Symptoms include:

+ Frequently binge-eating (eating more than you need for your height/weight in very little time; feeling a lack of control over what/how much you're eating)

+ Purging: either by misusing laxatives, diuretics or enemas, by fasting, excessive exercising or vomiting
+ If you binge-eat and carry out inappropriate compensatory behaviours, on average, at least twice a week for three months
+ You can't stop thinking about your body shape and weight

Eating disorders not otherwise specified (EDNOS): Eating disorders that are atypical; that is they don't exactly fit the description of anorexia nervosa or bulimia, but share some of the symptoms.

Examples include:

+ The criteria for anorexia nervosa are the same, except you still have regular periods
+ The criteria for anorexia nervosa are the same except that, despite considerable weight loss, your current weight is within the normal range
+ All the criteria for bulimia are met except you are binge-eating and purging less than twice a week or for less than three months
+ You are of normal body weight but you purge after eating small amounts of food (for example, self-induced vomiting after two biscuits)
+ You chew and spit out, but don't swallow, food
+ Having a binge-eating disorder: recurrent episodes of binge-eating but without any purging

See your GP if you're worried that you may be suffering from an eating disorder. You may also find the ideas and strategies in this book helpful alongside specialist treatment.

The deprivation cycle

It's common to characterise foods as 'good' and 'bad'. Whether these definitions come from a previous diet, cultural beliefs or something you once overheard, thinking of a certain food as bad/naughty/sinful is a one-way ticket to food preoccupation. By telling yourself that you can't eat something, you'll feel hard done by, you'll think more about it and you'll miss it when you don't have it. According to some unwritten rule, you can't have this, OK? Well, no. Who says? Before you know it, you're scoffing as much of it as you possibly can just to prove you're in charge. You think of nothing else when you're not eating it and then when you cave in, you'll eat twice as much because you know you won't be able to have it again. You tell yourself that this is the last time you'll succumb... but seeing as it is the last time, you might as well make the most of it.

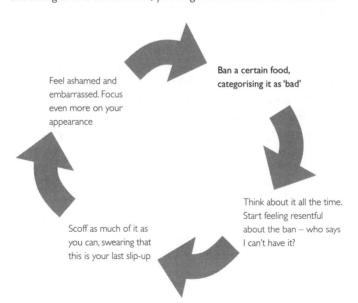

Ban a certain food, categorising it as 'bad'

Think about it all the time. Start feeling resentful about the ban – who says I can't have it?

Scoff as much of it as you can, swearing that this is your last slip-up

Feel ashamed and embarrassed. Focus even more on your appearance

The annoying thing is that when you eat a 'banned' food you never enjoy it. Oh, those few seconds it's in your mouth might give you a rush of satisfaction, but then the guilt and self-recrimination kick in.

Ⓢ Identifying your 'bad' foods

+ List any foods which you consider to be 'bad'; foods you would usually feel guilty about eating
+ Next, note down any times you're allowed to eat these foods, for example, carbs only before 6pm, chocolate when you're offered, sweets when you're alone
+ Finally, think about why these foods are 'bad'. Where did the impression that they're something to avoid or feel guilty about come from: a diet, your friends, your parents, an article?

Review: What's it like seeing your rules written down? Did you even realise you had 'bad' foods before now? Is there any science/proof to back up your categorisation or have you attributed an emotion to a food (guilt/shame) for no reason? For example, chocolate is commonly thought of as a treat, something decadent. However, it's only bad for you when you eat it excessively. By becoming more aware of your own food rules you can see how they're triggering certain emotions and unhelpful beliefs. Often our rules are very contradictory, for example that carbs are 'bad', even though you know scientifically they're good for you in moderation.

Ⓢ Scrap your 'bad' food list

+ Physically cross through your 'bad' food list. Go on, we'll wait
+ Start listening to your body. If you're hungry and your body wants chocolate, eat it, savour it and stop judging yourself. If you aren't hungry and don't want chocolate, then don't eat it. Start changing your relationship to food

Review: Not thinking of foods as 'bad' will allow you to truly enjoy them when you eat them, rather than gorging on them when you aren't really hungry and then feeling guilty. By de-mythicising them, you'll crave them less, think about them less and, no doubt, eat them less.

Next steps ...

Chapter 6 details your new healthy eating plan, which if you really throw yourself into it, will revolutionise (no exaggeration) your relationship with food.

Thoughts to take away

✓ Food can become the focus of appearance anxieties as it's something you can control and that can change your body. By re-assessing your food beliefs and behaviours you can foster a happier and healthier relationship with what you eat

✓ You can enjoy and savour food while still maintaining a healthy weight

✓ Dieting is nonsense. It doesn't work long-term and only aggravates your body image insecurities

6

A New Way
of Eating

Here we suggest a healthy eating plan for anyone who has issues about food or body shape. It's a truly sustainable way of breaking down negative thoughts, habits and emotional ties to food and to eating.

Building a better relationship with food

Our bodies are amazing, telling us what they need and when they need it – we've just forgotten how to listen to the signals or have become experts at ignoring them. If you start using your body as a guide to what, when and how to eat, rather than your mood or some stupid diet, you'll interrupt unhelpful and unhealthy thinking and behavioural cycles surrounding food. This plan will help you to either lose or gain weight if you need to, keeping you at a weight that's right for you.

Your new healthy eating plan

✦ Eat when you're hungry
✦ Eat what your body wants and needs to eat (no banned foods or special 'rules')
✦ Stop eating when you're full

That's it. It sounds so ridiculously simple, but ask yourself this, 'How often do I wait until I'm hungry before eating? How often do I eat what I really feel I want and need? How often do I stop when I'm full?' Hardly ever, right? If you're always on a diet you'll be abusing your hunger, seeing it as a badge of honour rather than a necessary message from your body. You'll also be restricting certain foods and basing a 'good' or 'bad' day on what your tape measure or scales say, leaving you both physically and mentally exhausted. And, if you're over-eating, you're abusing your body in another way, masking its natural signals with food.

This new eating plan is based on, and adapted from, the work of Susie Orbach, psychotherapist, social critic and expert on emotional and binge-eating. She believes your body knows best and that listening to it will make you feel healthy and in control. And she's right.

This new way of approaching food and eating will take some getting used to, but if you stick with it, it will break down habitual negative patterns and beliefs surrounding diet. Your current habits and beliefs have been ingrained for years and years, so of course it'll seem strange at first, but give it a go and you'll be amazed at the results. Learning to eat this way will:

+ Scrap your desire to go on faddy diets
+ Reduce the emotional pull of food
+ Stop self-recrimination cycles because no food is banned
+ Limit your preoccupation with food
+ Get you to a healthy weight that is sustainable

You'll start to trust yourself again around food because, unlike mind-bending diets, this is a change of lifestyle. It's better for you physically because you're working with your body rather than against it and better for you mentally as you're being proactive, without setting yourself up to pass or fail. You'll make informed choices about eating in a way that is sustainable in the long-term, rather than getting stuck in this cycle:

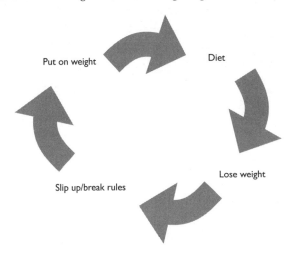

Put on weight

Diet

Slip up/break rules

Lose weight

Eat when you're hungry

When we eat there tends to be a trigger that pushes us towards the fridge:

+ **Environmental:** Smelling/seeing food, for example, walking past a cake shop, eating kids' leftovers or a colleague bringing doughnuts to work
+ **Biological:** Hunger, thirst, cravings
+ **Mental:** Thinking about food, remembering that half-eaten sandwich in the fridge, planning when and where you're next going to eat
+ **Emotional:** See Chapter 5
+ **Behavioural:** Eating on autopilot, for example, opening the fridge while waiting for the kettle to boil; always having a pudding when eating out; buying a pint and a packet of crisps; as a means of procrastination; having a snack at 3pm every day whether you're hungry or not
+ **Physical:** For example, eating because you're exhausted

⑤ Identifying your food triggers

Using the trigger list, fill in the table below during a normal day (a day when you're following your usual routine).

Day	What I ate (including time)	The trigger
Monday	9am: Poached eggs	Hunger (biological)
	11am: Toast and honey	Boredom (emotional)
	1pm: Soup and bread roll	Routine – it was officially 'lunch time' so I ate my lunch, even though I wasn't hungry (behavioural)
	3pm: Chocolate brownie	A colleague bought them into the office (environmental)
	5pm: Another chocolate brownie	Thought, 'Everyone else has had two' (mental)

Review: Did some of your triggers surprise you? Perhaps you weren't even aware there were triggers – you'd never considered it before, you just ate. By identifying your triggers you can become more aware of the process of eating, rather than just automatically reaching for food through habit or whenever you feel an urge.

We've put one of the examples into a mind map to show the connection between triggers, behaviour (eating), emotions, thoughts and body:

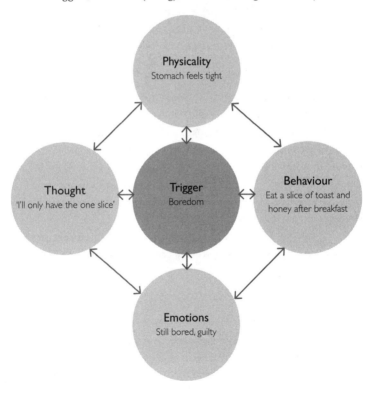

Physicality
Stomach feels tight

Thought
'I'll only have the one slice'

Trigger
Boredom

Behaviour
Eat a slice of toast and honey after breakfast

Emotions
Still bored, guilty

⑤ Your own 'trigger' mind map

Pick one of your triggers and fill out a mind map identifying the resulting thoughts, and physical and emotional responses to your eating (behaviour). If a thought was the trigger put 'thought/trigger' jointly in the centre.

Review: Becoming more conscious of these chain reactions means that when you next notice a trigger and find yourself about to eat automatically you can make a conscious decision whether to continue with your action or not. You're switching off autopilot and choosing whether to eat, fully aware of your potential emotional and physical reactions.

Tuning into hunger

To follow our healthy eating plan you need to tune into the hunger signals your body sends you and start making hunger your only eating trigger. We can confuse hunger with desire: you want to eat that buttery crumpet because it looks delicious, so you convince yourself that the pang of longing in your belly is hunger. It's not – it's just a pang of longing. It's important to learn to differentiate between hunger, desire and craving:

Hunger: A need to eat/need to fuel your body, driven by an empty sensation in your stomach

Desire: When you fancy eating something, but you're not actually hungry

Craving: A physiological/emotionally intense urge to eat (see pages 100–1)

Hunger changes according to the situation. For example, if you've been rushing around or exercising you'll be hungrier than if you spent the whole day watching TV because you've expended more energy. Your body will always let you know what it needs and when it needs it.

Hunger is one of your body's most important communication tools; it's not something to be feared or something to be abused. If you eat when you're hungry your metabolism will tick along at its optimum rate because it's getting what it needs when it needs it. You may find yourself eating more, but less regularly, or eating less, more regularly. It doesn't matter – you're not depriving your body of what it needs, you're listening to it and deliberately giving it what it's asking for. This means your metabolism won't slow down like it does on diets.

What does hunger feel like?

Everyone experiences hunger differently. Symptoms range from a rumbling stomach to full-blown headaches. We're going to rate hunger on a scale of 0–10, where 0 = totally stuffed, 5 = neutral and 10 = absolutely starving. Below are some example symptoms for each rating (but remember, everyone responds differently, so add your own descriptions/ delete the ones that don't apply):

0 Nauseated, stomach hurts from eating so much
1 Feel like a bowling ball is sitting in your belly
2 Have to loosen trousers/undo belt
3 Feel full, stomach feels 'tight'
4 Have eaten the right amount, feel comfortable
5 Neutral: not hungry, not full
6 Distracted, energy dip, small rumblings in stomach
7 Grumbly stomach, lack of concentration, low energy, mouth waters at thought of food
8 Growling stomach, feel a physical need to eat, experience hunger pangs
9 Shaky, can't concentrate on anything but food, beginnings of a headache
10 Raging headache, terrible mood, sluggish, stomach aching with hunger

ⓢ How do you experience hunger?
✦ Tomorrow, make it your mission to only eat when you're hungry. Work around any obstacles that might get in your way, such as if you have a

set lunch break at work, but aren't hungry when it arrives, buy a sandwich and eat it later during a five-minute break when you are. If you're going out for dinner with friends, don't eat for at least three hours before you go. We commonly start to experience hunger three to four hours since we last ate. How long does it take you to feel hungry?

✦ When you start feeling hungry, tune into the feeling: what sensations do you experience in your body? Where does the feeling start – your stomach, the back of your throat, in your chest? What happens when the feelings increase?

✦ Rate your feelings of hunger on the scale of 0–10

✦ When you reach a feeling of 6–7 eat! This isn't a competition to see how hungry you can get; it's a way of recognising your hunger symptoms so you know to eat when you're slightly or fairly hungry (a 6 or 7 on the hunger scale). Getting to 8–10 will mean you're more likely to overeat because you're too hungry

Review: If you're not sure whether you're hungry, chances are you're not, so wait until you're sure. If you find yourself thinking, 'I could really do with some brie and crackers right now' check in with your body to find out if the thought's caused by hunger, a desire or a craving. You can still eat what you desire, but just wait until you're actually hungry – it'll feel far more satisfying.

Eat what you want to eat

In Chapter 5 we asked you to strike out your 'bad foods' list so that they lose their emotional pull and you'll stop feeling guilty about eating them. Eating what you want to eat and ditching all the conditions associated with certain foods is a key part of this plan. Instead, you should eat whatever your body tells you to eat. If you only eat foods that are 'allowed' according to some ingrained belief system, you won't get much

The basic rules of eating when you're hungry

+ Eat when you reach a 6 or 7 (see page 97) on your hunger scale, regardless of when you last ate
+ Don't skip meals if you're hungry and don't push your hunger past 8 as your metabolism will slow down if it feels it's starving
+ Work around any obstacles that might stop you eating when you're hungry
+ Eat what you want to eat (see left and below)
+ Stop when you're full (see page 103)

satisfaction from any foods because you'll feel restricted. You're taking the pleasure out of eating and eating is such a big part of your life, why not make it as nice as possible?

Obviously some foods are better for you than others, so it's all about listening to your body. We're not advocating wolfing down an entire tub of ice cream every time you're hungry because your body wouldn't like that. Instead, you need to work out what foods your body likes and needs. Visit www.nhs.uk/livewell and www.bbcgoodfood.com for information on nutrition and food types.

Ⓢ Your food pleasure log

+ For the next week only eat when you're hungry. Eat whatever you want to eat – what you think your body wants and what you desire/crave
+ Fill in the table on the next page, monitoring what you ate, what the trigger was (be honest if you didn't just eat when you were hungry), whether it was fuelled by a desire or a craving and how you felt physically during and after eating. We've filled in some examples:

Day	What I ate (including time)	Trigger (i.e. emotional/ behavioural and whether it was a desire or a craving)	Physical response when eating and afterwards
Monday	7.30am: Bowl of cereal	Hunger	Feel satisfied both during eating and afterwards
	9am: Muffin	Caught my eye at the coffee shop (desire)	Tasted great while eating, but then I felt heavy
	1pm: Jacket potato with cheese and beans	I was hungry and really fancied it (hunger and desire)	Tasted lovely, but at 3pm I felt bloated and a bit drowsy

+ At the end of the week make a note of all the foods that made you feel uncomfortable physically and all the foods that made you feel great
+ When you ate foods that made you feel uncomfortable, did your body want them or was your choice fuelled by a desire/craving (see box)

Review: We all have foods that are a good fit for us and foods that aren't. This exercise is a way to start noticing how food makes you feel physically. Your body might react to certain foods, making you feel bloated, hyper, lethargic or bring you out in a rash. For example, chocolate can make you feel great for a bit, but eat too much and you can feel heavy – even nauseous. Foods making you feel that way should be eaten in moderation.

Cravings

Ever been sitting at your desk and suddenly the image of The Perfect Cheeseburger wafts into your mind and you can't think of anything else? Or a piece of succulent sushi. Or a slice of banana cake. Whatever it is, you need it right now. Nothing else will do. Sound familiar? Well, that's a craving.

∵ Cravings are a physiological and emotionally intense urge to eat, generally occurring when you're not hungry. The brain tends to associate food with reward and for many of us cravings kick in when we're stressed or anxious. A study by University of California found that stressed-out rats 'craved' sugar and fat; when they ate it their brains produced less of the hormones that trigger the fight or flight reflex, proving cravings are both physiologically and emotionally driven.

What you crave is totally individual, but the majority of us hanker after high-fat, high-sugar foods. This is down to both chemical reactions in our brains (fatty, sugary foods release feel-good chemicals into the bloodstream) and psychological influences, for example, stress, boredom or nostalgia for a certain food.

Cravings can lead to self-recrimination and regret. The more you get used to identifying them, the better you'll get at challenging them: 'Do I need this?'; 'Will I feel better or worse after I've eaten it?' Cut down the number of times you give into cravings by telling yourself you won't give into them when you're not hungry, but can treat yourself when you are. Cravings will go away quicker if you have a plan for how to deal with them, rather than if you're undecided. As soon as you start to 'um' and 'er' they'll leap on your indecision. Distract yourself by making a cup of tea, doing a puzzle or reading a few pages of your book.

An easy tip: If you crave sugar eat dessert before the rest of your meal – you won't feel you're depriving yourself and the savoury food that comes next will squash the craving.

Eating mindfully

How often do you find yourself reaching for another crisp/biscuit/peanut before realising the packet's finished? We eat lunch at our desks, grab sandwiches on the move and eat dinner in front of the TV. Eating chaotically is the norm and we rarely taste what we put in our mouths.

Being mindful means being present in the moment, aware of what's going on in your head, your body and the world around you. Eating mindfully is paying attention to your food and the process of eating and nothing else – not your emails, your phone, your good-looking colleague or a TV show. It's a way of really tuning into your body, and, once you're proficient at it, you can go back to reading, working, watching telly at the same time because you'll be more adept at truly savouring your food.

⑤ Eating mindfully

+ Over the next week, try eating one meal a day mindfully
+ Simply eat. Sit down (most impulse-eating is done standing up, so by sitting down you're making a conscious decision to eat), turn off your phone/computer/TV and concentrate on your food. This is best done in silence, so avoid trying it at dinner parties
+ As you eat focus on:
    + What you see: the textures and colours of the food
    + What you smell
    + How your body reacts in anticipation of the food
    + How it feels when you place the food in your mouth
    + How it tastes when you bite into it, for example, the juiciness of a piece of fruit, the spiciness of a curry, the strong flavour of a herb
    + What you can hear, for example, crunching, fizzing, snapping
    + How it feels when you swallow and how your body reacts to the anticipation of the next mouthful

Taking time to sit down and eat may feel like a luxury you can't afford, but compare that to how much time you spend thinking/worrying/fretting about how you look or what you're 'allowed' to eat – half an hour a day is nothing compared to that, right?

Review: Eating mindfully will completely change your relationship to food, making you feel calmer and more in control. It will stop impulse-eating and eating on autopilot. You'll also know once and for all whether you're actually enjoying the food you're eating – if you're not, stop and eat something else!

Stop when you're full

This is the final piece of the puzzle. If you eat when you're hungry and pay attention to the pleasure of eating (by eating mindfully), your body will let you know when it's full. This will only work if you eat when you're hungry, though. If you chow down on a sandwich when you're not hungry there was never a biological reason to start eating, making it much harder to know when to stop.

Being full isn't eating to the point where you have to undo your trousers or be carried out of a restaurant in a fireman's lift. Ideally, you should feel satisfied and still able to go for a brisk walk. If this doesn't sound realistic, you're probably used to over-eating and so your idea of fullness has become distorted. It's time to tune into what's actually happening within your body.

Research shows that it takes about 20 minutes between your stomach filling up to your brain receiving the message that you're full. When we eat quickly our body doesn't have time to register that it's full before you're moving on to second helpings. Eating mindfully will help to slow down the eating process, giving time for the 'I'm full' alert to reach your brain. A recent Japanese study of 1,700 women found that eating more slowly resulted in feeling fuller sooner (or registering that you were full sooner) and so the participants ended up eating less. If you're full you're not depriving yourself because you don't need more food.

⑤ Am I full yet?

+ Sit down and eat mindfully. Chew each bite and take time over your food
+ Pay attention to your body, tuning into signals that you're getting fuller
+ Eat what you think is the right amount (judging by how you feel physically, rather than what's left on your plate) and then stop, leave the table and go and do something else
+ After 20 minutes check in with your body: are you still hungry? If so, what are you hungry for? Feel free to go and eat it! Then start the cycle again. Stop when you feel full. Wait 20 minutes and check in again
+ If you're eating with other people, eat what you believe to be 'enough' and then wait for 20 minutes. Meals with others are rarely rushed, so take your time: talk, put your knife and fork down and drink your wine. If, after the plates are cleared, you're still hungry, order a dessert
+ If you're still not sure how you personally experience fullness, focus on the following questions:
    + Where do you start to experience fullness in your body: your stomach, your throat, your chest?
    + What sensations are you experiencing: a tightening of skin around the stomach? A heavy feeling in your lower abdomen?
    + Rate your fullness on the same hunger scale we used before: 0 = totally stuffed, 5 = neutral and 10 = starving. Aim to stop eating at 3 or 4, where you feel full, but comfortable

Review: Are you better at identifying fullness now you're more familiar with identifying hunger? It can be hard to stop eating even when you know you're full for several reasons, which we discuss next.

How we see our food

There really is some truth to the saying 'Your eyes are bigger than your stomach'. When we eat, we generally assess how full we are by what's left on our plate, rather than by how we feel physically. It's common to be guided by sight as food is often determined by volume, for example, a packet of crisps, a meal for two or a plateful of food. You're given a certain amount, so that's how much you eat, regardless of how hungry or full you are. Faced with a portion of food twice as big as you'd normally consume, you're likely to eat a third more than normal. In a study conducted at a health and fitness camp, campers served larger bowls consumed 16 per cent more cereal than those given smaller bowls and, despite the fact that they were eating more, they estimated their consumption to be 7 per cent lower than the other group. This shows that not only do large portions mean we eat more, but large plates trick us into thinking we're eating less.

Managing over-eating

Here are some common reasons for over-eating and effective ways of challenging them:

+ It would be rude to leave it: Just explain you're full, but that the food was delicious. Look around you – other people leave food and it's fine
+ I paid for it, I should eat it: Ask for a take-away box to take home the leftovers – enjoy them tomorrow!
+ It tastes so good: You can have it again another time – this isn't the last time you're ever going to be able to eat this meal
+ There are starving children in Africa: This has absolutely no bearing on your dinner right here, right now
+ My parents used to/still punish me if I didn't/don't finish everything on my plate: If you still live with your parents ask for less to start with

so you can finish everything and not over-eat; if you're an independent adult then you're allowed to make your own rules now, yes?

✦ I'll be too busy to eat later: Take a snack in your bag in case you get hungry

✦ I fear hunger: Keep snacks with you to eat when you do feel hungry and remind yourself that you can access food when you need it. The only way to puncture your fear is to disprove it by following this strategy and realising that experiencing gentle hunger isn't dangerous

Ⓢ Learning you don't have to eat everything

✦ Every day next week, leave something unfinished: a crisp in the packet, some popcorn at the bottom of the box, a chunk of your chocolate biscuit. Throw it away, give it away or save it for later

✦ If you find this hard, take more food than normal to start with to purposefully leave (don't just eat this too!) – just to prove you can leave something

✦ Notice habits that encourage you to eat and work around them. For example, instead of leaving leftover pasta within easy picking distance, put it away in the fridge so you actively have to open the fridge, undo the container and choose to eat more rather than nibble on autopilot

Review: This will build up your resistance to the embedded illusion that you have to finish everything you start eating. You don't! You don't have to finish everything on your plate and you don't have to eat every single thing you fancy. The more you do this the more you'll strengthen your resolve to only eat what you need.

Top tips for combating over-eating

✦ Don't over-fill your plate. The size of the plate should not dictate the size of your meal. If you find that it does, consider investing in smaller-sized plates

✦ Buy one packet of crisps rather than a family-sized bag. Buy a four-pack of yoghurt rather than one big pot

✦ Mix up what you have for lunch. Always going to the same place will mean you order the same thing and will therefore be tempted to eat as much as you always do ('but I always finish this sandwich'). Going somewhere new will kick-start new habits. The same goes if you always take the same packed lunch into work each day – take something new

✦ If you do over-eat don't beat yourself up about it. It's not the end of the world. Just start again with your next meal

Food for thought (literally)

Your thoughts play a dastardly role in both triggering and maintaining negative eating behaviours. It's important to be aware of them so they don't trick you into ignoring or dismissing your new eating plan.

Common thoughts associated with food include:

✦ I deserve it/It's a celebration/It'd be rude not to eat it
✦ But this diet promises to work!
✦ The food will only go to waste
✦ One won't matter
✦ I can't eat that
✦ I shouldn't have eaten that
✦ I'll just have one
✦ I'll make up for it later
✦ I need rules to follow

- ✦ It doesn't count if no one sees me eat it
- ✦ It's free/I've already paid for it
- ✦ It'll make me feel better
- ✦ I've already eaten badly so today doesn't count
- ✦ I don't care

Now we challenge some of these thoughts:

Situation	Thought	Challenge
Wanting to lose weight quickly	'But this diet promises to work!'	Diets don't work long-term. You're just prolonging your negative preoccupations with food. Eating sensibly is all you have to do to find and maintain a healthy weight – one that's right for you
	'I need to have a strict set of rules to follow'	Rules set you up for failure and make the foods you can't have more enticing. By changing your relationship with food and listening to your body you'll have more success long-term
Seeing someone who's slim	'I could never look like that'	Who cares? You're you and they're them. You're not the same person. You look great – seriously. You just need the confidence to see it. If you felt healthier, you'd feel more beautiful
Seeing food you want when you're not hungry	'I'll just have one'	Yeah, and then feel bad about it so you eat another one as a big 'sod you' to the food gods
	'I'm bored and it will only go to waste'	You'll still be bored after you've finished eating and you could always eat it later when you're actually hungry

These kinds of thoughts have the potential to trigger your self-recrimination cycle. If you want a slice of cake when you're not hungry as a treat, go for it, but only if you don't then punish yourself for it. You're allowed treats, but make them the exception rather than the rule.

The 80:20 rule

Apply the 80:20 rule when it comes to your life. Aim to live well 80 per cent of the time and allow yourself 20 per cent worth of slack. No one's perfect and being healthy shouldn't ever become something else to stress about.

Thoughts to take away

✓ Eating when you're hungry and stopping when you're full is a simple way of overhauling any negative associations, behaviours, thoughts and emotions you have around food

✓ It's a way of tuning into your body so you're more aware of what it wants and needs rather than being oblivious to it or ignoring it

✓ Your thoughts will try to trip you up – challenging them will make you feel more in control about your choices

7

The Think Tank

Your thoughts like to play tricks on you, making you believe certain things are facts when (in fact) they're just negatively skewed opinions. Understanding the games your mind plays will give you distance from these thoughts so you can decide whether they're worthy of your time.

Mind games

Thoughts are wily rogues. They can trip you up, make you feel bad and convince you they have your best interests at heart when they don't. When you feel low, your mind tries to find reasons to explain your emotions so it actively looks for 'proof' to substantiate your fears and insecurities, for example, 'You feel unattractive because you messed up your diet'. It also dredges up memories of times you felt similarly ('This is just like when…'), making you feel worse. It's not doing this because it's evil, it's doing it because it's looking for 'threats' as part of the in-built danger-detection system you were born with (fight or flight). It believes by looking for bad things you'll be forearmed against them, without taking into account that you'll feel terrible and will mistake the thoughts for facts – 'He is laughing at my new haircut'; 'I am too fat'; 'My boobs are too big/small' – affecting your behaviour, emotions and body and making you feel less than beautiful.

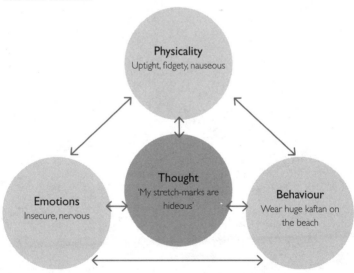

Thinking is automatic, like breathing – you just do it. If you're constantly thinking bad thoughts, you'll feel rubbish – it makes sense. The trick is to start stepping back from your thoughts and seeing them as things that can be challenged. Your thoughts aren't true just because you thought them – they're opinions that can be investigated and confronted. Your thoughts don't define you; they don't make you who you are.

Thought processing and attentional bias

Thought processing is the process that drives your inner autopilot function. To manage the volume of information you take in every day, your brain chooses what to flag up to your consciousness so your head can cope. For example, you don't think about the process of brushing your teeth: 'I'll put the toothpaste on the brush, lift the brush to my mouth, open my lips, put the brush in' and all the rest – you just do it. This is down to thought processing, where activities become automatic so your mind can think about other, more important, things. Unfortunately, negative thought processes can become automatic too, including body image anxieties, e.g. automatically looking at your bingo wings in photos. Your mind becomes trained to automatically focus on gloomy things, such as what you consider to be your less attractive features. This is known as 'attentional bias' – you're so busy focusing on your enormous chunky elephant feet that you lose all sense of reality or perspective and dismiss anything positive. People who feel confident in their body will do the opposite, focusing on their best features and paying attention to compliments. For those with serious, life-affecting body image anxieties, diets or surgery won't make any long-term difference to how they feel emotionally as their attentional bias is still switched to 'negative' so they'll just hunt for something new to feel bad about.

It's natural to pay attention to criticisms or judgements. We have a human desire to 'fit in' and so want to protect ourselves from rejection.

However, it's when you focus only on the bad things that there's a problem. For example, if you get four compliments on your new haircut, but one person doesn't mention it, you'll wonder why they didn't. Did they prefer your old cut? Perhaps you were wrong to cut it? This kind of thinking becomes so ingrained, you don't even realise how crazy it is. Four people loved your hair; one person didn't. If you were being fair, you'd spend 80 per cent of the time thinking about the compliments and 20 per cent thinking about the lack of comment, but it never seems to work out that way. You start observing yourself as you think others see you – as if you're them, sneering in disgust – and you'll even start assessing neutral events as hostile like, 'They're talking about how disgusting I look'.

🅢 Don't look, don't find

+ Tonight, pick up your notebook and ask yourself (this will seem random, but bear with us), 'How many For Sale signs did I see today?' Note down the rough estimate
+ Tomorrow, actively look for For Sale signs wherever you go. Tally them up in your notebook as you go along
+ If you're not in an area where there are many For Sale signs, change what you look out for (maybe cats, red cars or kids on scooters)

Review: You'll no doubt see loads more For Sale signs on the day you actively looked for them than on the day you weren't even thinking about them. This isn't because it was National House Selling Day, it's because you were actively hunting them out – just like you actively hunt out criticisms and things that make you feel bad about your body and your appearance.

Standing up to Negative Automatic Thoughts (NATs)

NATs are thoughts that whizz into your head without you even realising. They are the thoughts that masquerade as facts: 'I look awful'; 'I need to look like him/her'; 'No one will fancy me because of how I look'. They are pessimistic appraisals and interpretations that you accept as truths without even really hearing them. NATs back up the beliefs you have about yourself so they seem plausible even though they're unreasonable and unrealistic.

NATs can become part of your internal dialogue without you even realising and they can often spiral out of control, with one turning into two, three or four, like Chinese Whispers:

'I've put on a bit of weight' → 'Everyone's looking at my stomach' → 'Only beautiful people get any positive attention' → 'I didn't get that job because I'm fat' → 'I'm a failure in life'

Your original worry ('I've put on a bit of weight') bears no resemblance to the all-encompassing feeling of doom and gloom you end up with ('I'm a failure in life'), but you've lost all perspective because the NATs have convinced you they're reasonable and factual.

As your mind builds a story to explain what's going on and why you feel the way you do, it gets harder to separate genuine fact from fiction. Any information that doesn't fit your mind's story is ignored or dismissed as irrelevant. You start wallowing in your fears, dwelling on the past and worrying about the future until you feel inhibited and insecure. If you were fairer to yourself, you'd feel happier and therefore more beautiful. However, at the moment your mind is trained to tell sad stories and encourage NATs. You need to learn how to assess them objectively so you can gain a realistic interpretation of a situation.

The most common types of NAT

The following list comprises the most common categories of NAT, with Golden Rules for combating them. Learning these types will make it easier for you to identify them when they gallop through your head, so you can stop negative repercussions on your behaviour, mood and body. Being able to categorise your NATs will reassure you that these are just nasty bullying thoughts, not generally accepted truths.

Often we try to suppress bad thoughts, making them stronger. For example, if we told you not to, under any circumstances, picture a pink horse you'd immediately think of a pink horse. It's just the way the mind works. If you're desperately trying not to think about something you'll only ensure you think about it more. By confronting your thoughts they won't be able to haunt you; they'll simply move on.

Monochrome

You see things in black or white, all or nothing, with no middle ground. You set yourself near-impossible tasks with strict parameters of success and failure, for example, 'My appearance has and will hold me back in life' or 'If I eat that slice of cake I'm pathetic'.

Golden Rule: There is always a middle ground, a grey area, another side to the story. There's never any 'pass' or 'fail' where body image is concerned. Cut yourself some slack, try to find alternative views to your rigid perspective and reward yourself when you achieve things rather than constantly moving the goalposts.

Telepathic trickery

You believe you can read minds: 'He's judging me' or 'She'll think I'm rude if I don't eat her biscuits'. You second-guess people without realising that this is unfair to both you and to them.

Golden Rule: People generally aren't that interested in everyone else. Just like you, other people are usually caught up in their own dramas. You can't read minds and even if you could you'd be surprised by how far off-base your assumptions are. Stop projecting your insecurities onto other people; it's not fair. If you really want to know what they're thinking, ask them.

Fortune-teller error

You predict the future using extreme measures of success and failure, such as, 'My boyfriend will dump me if he sees me without make-up'. These predictions can turn into self-fulfilling prophecies: you hide your face from your boyfriend and constantly tell him how awful you look. He does end up running for the hills – but because of your behaviour, not your appearance.

Golden Rule: You can't predict the future, just as you can't read minds. The only way to take the sting out of these predictions is to challenge them by testing out alternative views (see Chapter 9) or stop making them altogether.

Overgeneralisation

You see a single negative event as a never-ending pattern. Didn't ask that girl out? That's because you never ask people out. Didn't like the photo of you in the company brochure? That's because you always look bad in photos.

Golden Rule: Change 'never' and 'always' to 'not this time' or 'sometimes'.

Nit-picking

You pick out a single negative detail and dwell on it exclusively, thus losing any perspective on the event as a whole. It's like finding a loose thread on your favourite jumper and hating your entire wardrobe. For example, 'He complimented my new dress, but not my hair because it's so thin'.

Golden Rule: Put things in perspective and don't invent criticisms. If 99 per cent of something is good and 1 per cent bad or neutral, focus 99 per cent of your attention on the good things and 1 per cent on the rest.

Positive discrimination

You discount any positive information or twist it to fit your negative view, for example, 'They were only saying I looked nice to be polite'.

Golden Rule: Learning to accept compliments is a sign of confidence and self-acceptance. Appreciate that good things do happen and that your downer view of yourself isn't right, true or fair.

Catastrophising

You make a situation seem worse than it really is, jumping to terrible conclusions and worrying about the future. For example, 'I can't bear this craving', 'This is going to be a disaster', 'I'll never get over it if I fail.' **Golden Rule:** Ask yourself, 'What's the worst that could happen? If it does, can I cope? What's realistically the most likely scenario and what's the best outcome?' Have faith in your ability to deal with tough situations and to see things through.

I'm sad, therefore everything is sad

You assume that your negative emotions reflect the way things really are, even though objective evidence says otherwise. For example, 'I feel awful, therefore I must be awful', or in Megan's case (see example on pages 120–1), 'I'm intimidated by that girl, therefore I can't be as good as her'. **Golden Rule:** Your mood can't shape the future or make facts out of opinions. What you do dictates what happens to you, so don't let your feelings influence your world view or your behaviour.

Shoulda, woulda, coulda

You try to motivate yourself with 'shoulds' and 'shouldn'ts', as if you need to be whipped or punished. For example, 'I shouldn't have eaten that. I should have worn my other pair of jeans. I shouldn't have gone out without make-up on.' 'Should' suggests an external restriction, something you should do according to an invisible rule book, and restrictions make you feel beaten down, initiating the fail/pass self-recrimination cycle. **Golden Rule:** Change the word 'should' to the far more positive 'would/

will' or 'could/can' so the thought becomes 'I will eat that when I'm hungry. I will wear my other jeans next time. I can and will go out without make-up.'

Why always me?

You believe negative events result from your own physical flaws, for example, 'He didn't speak to me because he thinks I look awful', 'The girls didn't want to get ready for the party together because they didn't want to see my skin grafts'.

Golden Rule: Remember: it's not all about you. Low mood is making you paranoid, focusing on often-unrealistic false 'threats'. Next time you assume the worst about yourself, or take responsibility for events, remove the 'you' aspect and look again: 'Perhaps he didn't talk to me because he was on the phone'; 'Perhaps it was easier for us to get ready separately.'

Typecasting

Slapping yourself with a nasty label that you believe sums you up: 'hideous', 'disgusting', 'a lard-arse'. On the end-of-film credits reel, that's how you would be described: 'Ugly witch played by [insert own name].'

Golden Rule: Ask yourself 'Would I categorise a friend in this way?' No! (If you would, then you're not much of a friend.) 'Do I sum up other people – their characters, personalities, looks and behaviour – with a single word or phrase?' No. 'Do I really believe other people think of me by this description?' No. So why are you doing this to yourself? Extend yourself the same respect as you do other people.

Ⓢ Identifying your most common NATs

✦ For the next week, whenever you notice a NAT pinging through your mind jot it down in the table on the next page, identify its type (i.e. typecasting or catastrophising), how it made you feel emotionally and what it made you do or think about doing

Thought	Thought category	Emotion	Behaviour
'She only said I look nice because she feels sorry for me'	Positive discrimination	Unhappy, resigned	Hide away to avoid attention
'He won't notice my new haircut because he can't see past my weight'	Fortune-teller error	Ashamed, embarrassed	Wear baggy, dark clothes, put hair up to hide haircut
'I'm so disgusting'	Typecasting	Guilty, ashamed	Act sullen and uninterested in other people
'Everyone wishes they had pretty Janice on their team rather than me'	Telepathic trickery	Angry, jealous	Snappy and stand-offish

Review: Identifying the specific category of NAT that bothers you will make you more aware of negative patterns. You may be particularly susceptible to one type and so can start digging deeper: 'Why do I always catastrophise?' Becoming more aware of your personal response to body image anxieties will give you more options for making changes. Once you're aware of what's happening you can choose how to proceed: 'I know I'm having a typecasting thought. Shall I indulge or ignore it?'

Example: A tough interview

Megan was waiting outside the office where she'd be having the second interview for a great job. The first interview had gone really well and she got on brilliantly with the woman who would be her new boss. Nervous, but excited, she'd arrived 20 minutes early. Five minutes before her slot, the door to the office opened and a stunning woman walked out. She had jet-black hair, tattoos all the way up her arms and was wearing a sleek 1950s-style suit and four-inch heels. Megan watched open-mouthed as she walked off.

> ⋯⟩ 'Wow, I can't possibly compete with her,' she thought. 'She's clearly far cooler and more interesting than me. My suit is boring, I'm wearing old flat shoes and you can see my spots under my fringe. I'm never going to get this job.'

Megan's mind map looked like this:

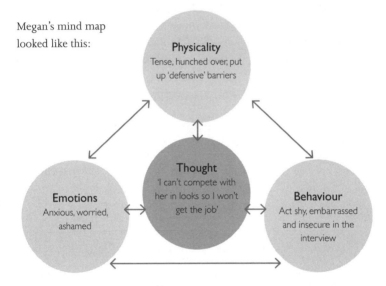

Physicality
Tense, hunched over, put up 'defensive' barriers

Thought
'I can't compete with her in looks so I won't get the job'

Emotions
Anxious, worried, ashamed

Behaviour
Act shy, embarrassed and insecure in the interview

Megan's NATs were complete drivel. If she'd been able to step back from them and see them for what they were (thoughts, not facts), she would have been able to challenge them: 'Of course I can compete with her – that's why I'm here. I've already got through to the final round, so clearly I have something to offer. Aren't I being unfair on myself, the other candidate and on the interviewers by assuming she's got this far on the basis of her looks? I actually like my suit and I can't walk in heels, so would look like an idiot trying to.'

❺ Challenging your NATs

+ The next time you have a NAT, catch it and challenge it, like Megan did
+ Fill out the table below with the original NAT and how much you believed it on a scale of 0–100 per cent (where 0 = not at all and 100 = totally convinced)
+ Jot down how the thought affected you emotionally
+ Next, challenge the thought. Ask yourself, 'Is this really true? Is there a fairer and more realistic way of looking at this?' Really throw as much energy into combating the thought as you usually do in finding evidence to back it up
+ Finally, assess how much you believe the original NAT now after your challenges (0–100 per cent)

We have filled out some examples:

Thought	Emotion	Challenge	New emotion
'Everyone's thinking I look awful' (belief in thought: 80%)	Nervous, ashamed	Is everyone thinking it? How do I know – have I asked them all? Can I read minds? Didn't someone compliment me this morning?	Calmer (belief in original thought: 30%)
'Life would be easier if I lost weight' (belief in thought: 100%)	Unhappy, frustrated	What parts of my life does weight affect directly? (Be honest – probably nowhere near as much as you're currently blaming it for.) Does everyone who's slim have an easy life or do they have problems too? Do people who are my weight have good jobs/ nice partners/great lives?	Better, a bit happier, less angry at myself (belief in original thought: 60%)

Review: Filling out the table is good practice for challenging NATs and will make you realise how often they rampage through your mind, doing untold damage. It's also a good way of starting to see patterns in NATs – do they all involve weight, work, friends, your partner? You can then start seeing whether there's a bigger issue driving them.

Thoughts are just thoughts

Just like your looks, your thoughts don't define you. They don't make you who you are. They are events that happen in your mind that can be acted upon or ignored. Accepting this is a huge relief – you're not beholden to your thoughts, you can choose whether to believe them or whether to challenge them. The next strategy is a way of distancing yourself from them so you become more aware of them as mental events that come and go. It's a very effective form of mindfulness that will stop you getting caught up in a thought whirlwind, feeling bad and then acting out. Instead, you can step back from them and start exerting some control.

Ⓢ Thought leaves

+ Imagine yourself on a river bank watching the river run past. The sun sparkles on the water as it flows quickly over small pebbles and rocks
+ You notice an oak tree hanging over the river. As you watch a leaf falls off and drifts down, landing gently on the water before floating away downstream
+ As the next leaf falls, put a thought that's been distressing you onto the leaf, without thinking about it or analysing it
+ Watch it hit the water and float away
+ As the next leaf falls do the same – put a thought on it and watch it disappear

Review: Yes, this might seem crazy if you've never practised mindfulness before, but put aside your scepticism and try it for 10 minutes every day this week. If you really go for it and put each internal criticism, worry, anxiety and NAT on a leaf before watching them float away, you will feel calmer and more in control of what's going on in your mind.

This strategy is a way of accepting that thoughts are just thoughts – they come and go like leaves floating on a river or trains at a station. Imagine it: a train comes rocketing into the station, destination: Insecurity Central. Normally, you'd leap on board grasping your one-way ticket, or worse, throw yourself in front of it. By stepping back from the train-thoughts and watching them come and go, you're exercising control over whether or not you engage with them. '

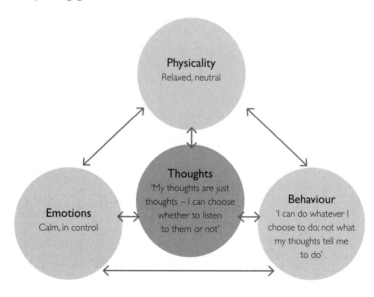

Thoughts to take away

✓ If you stop actively looking for and concentrating on things that make you feel bad you'll feel happier, calmer and more in control

✓ Learning to identify NATs will rob them of their power as you'll know the type of game they're playing

✓ Thoughts are transient mental events that you can choose to engage with or ignore

8

Judgement Day

Your judgemental inner critic likes nothing better than to heckle you and put you down. Here we'll teach you how to shut him/her up by learning how to accept compliments, reward yourself for your achievements, disregard unfair comparisons and be kinder to yourself.

Thought crimes

That little voice in your head that puts you down, tells you you're ugly and heckles you whenever you try to defend yourself is your 'inner critic'. Picture the person you always try to avoid talking to at parties, the one who thinks relentless moaning, whining and gossiping makes good conversation and who is an expert at backhanded compliments ('My dad has those jeans', 'I tried on that dress, but it was too baggy around the waist'). You have a miniature version of that person in your head. How delightful! They're prejudiced against you and constantly spout NATs, ignore compliments, compare you negatively to everyone and dwell on the past – all thought crimes we're going to teach you to fight.

Thought Crime 1: Ignoring, dismissing or explaining away compliments

When you have poor body image your mind is negatively programmed to spotlight the bad things and ignore, dismiss or explain away compliments: 'They only said that out of pity'; 'Did they say I looked nice because I look horrible the rest of the time?' Your inner critic keeps your self-belief levels so painfully low you genuinely won't see any truth in admiration or praise.

To build a more positive and realistic view of yourself as a whole person (not just a selection of physical parts) you need to start giving yourself compliments and accepting them from others. By starting to acknowledge your good bits, you're tipping the scales of self-evaluation back into balance.

⑤ Your objective appraisal
Part 1

✦ Make a list of your positive personality traits (not physical traits) in your notebook, including all your character strengths, talents and achievements. Are you loyal, hardworking, witty, caring, interested in others, a good cook?

+ If you're struggling, use these questions as a guide:
    + What do I like about who I am?
    + What am I good at?
    + What do others say they like about me or that I'm good at?
    + What are my favourite hobbies?
    + What compliments have I received recently?
    + How do I overcome challenges?
    + Have I helped anyone with anything lately?
    + What attributes do I appreciate in others that I might also possess?
+ Next, ask a friend, partner or family member what they like best about you. Ask someone you trust and explain why you're doing it, so you're not too intimidated

Part 2

+ Now, go and stand in front of a full-length mirror, take a deep breath and look at yourself objectively, as if you're looking at a stranger
+ Pick out three positive parts of this 'stranger's' body. What are their three best physical features? Do they have lovely hands, beautiful eyes, long eyelashes, a toned physique or nice hair?
+ DON'T start qualifying these positives with negatives, such as, 'They have lovely hair, but I'm not sure about the colour'. You're only allowed to think of the good things. If you still find this tough, list the three least-terrible things, such as, 'Well, I suppose their nose is OK'. (Isn't it strange how you'd never struggle to pick three good features on an actual stranger?)
+ Once you have your top three, step away from the mirror and write them down into your notebook

Review: Listing your best personality/character traits will force you to acknowledge your good bits – you do have them, contrary to what your inner critic tells you – and focus on something other than appearance. Writing these points down means you're taking them seriously. This isn't in any way arrogant, it's healthy. You're just balancing up a way of thinking that's skewed. Spending time thinking only of good things about yourself will lift your mood and put you in a better frame of mind to think more positively about your appearance (part 2 of the strategy). Hopefully you found it easier than you perhaps suspected it might be to then find three things you quite like about your body. The next time you feel insecure, look at this list of your best bits. You wrote them down, so they're true.

Thought Crime 2: Comparing yourself negatively to others

It's human nature to draw comparisons; it's part of our in-built survival-of-the-fittest drive. We compare everything: exes, restaurants, films and clothes. However, the thing we most love to compare is how we measure up against others. This is called social comparison and there are two types: upward and downward. Upward social comparison is when you measure yourself against those you perceive to be better off, while downward is against those you believe are worse off. For example, comparing yourself physically to a world-famous athlete would be classed as upward social comparison, while comparing yourself physically to the wicked witch in a fairy tale or professionally to your subordinate would be downward.

While comparing yourself to others is totally natural, problems occur when you only ever engage in upward social comparison, constantly measuring yourself against those you see as better off. This erodes your self-esteem as you'll always find yourself lacking. Your attentional bias will kick in and dismiss any information that counters your view, for example, 'James is much better looking and more successful than me', discounting the fact that he's up to his ears in debt. Or, 'Zoe always gets more attention from guys than I do', discounting the fact that she's in an awful relationship that makes her miserable.

Body image anxieties invite upward social comparisons that aren't realistic and that don't take in the full story. OK, so Natasha does have better skin than you, but she really covets your bright green eyes. And, yes, that actress does look fantastic, but so would you if you had her on-call personal trainers, sushi chefs and make-up artists.

You also might find yourself comparing how you look now to how you looked in the past, such as 'I'm so much fatter now'. Any information that serves to put you in a better position ('but I have a better job/relationship/financial situation/friends now') is ignored.

Our visual culture means we're constantly bombarded by images that invite upward social comparisons, fuelling body image anxieties: snaps of celebrities on the beach, 'aspirational' adverts, 'get your dream body' features and holiday photos, party pics and 'selfies' on social media sites. Research proves that constantly rating yourself against others (or yourself in the past) increases body image anxieties, so it's integral for your mental health that you actively search for realistic and fair comparisons.

Ⓢ Curbing comparisons

+ The next time you find yourself comparing yourself negatively, STOP. Ask yourself: 'Am I being fair on myself and them? Do I know the full story?' Then actively look for something positive in your life/looks/job. Refer back to the list you made of your best bits in the previous strategy

+ Pay attention to the triggers that initiate these bouts of comparison, such as looking at images of celebrities or reading about diets – then stop doing them!

+ Cut down or cut out social media. Looking at images of other people or analysing your own 'flaws' in pictures will feed your anxieties. As soon as you can look at pictures dispassionately, log back on, but until then don't give yourself the chance to feel bad. (We bet you'll be amazed at how much more positive you feel after just two days of not checking.)

✦ Distract yourself (make a cup of tea, read a book, call a friend) or use the present moment focus training strategy (see pages 139–41) to draw your focus away from these thoughts

Review: Now you're aware of it, are you surprised at how often you compare yourself to others? Often we do it unconsciously, so we have no idea how much we're putting ourselves down, just accepting the thoughts as facts ('She's prettier than me'; 'He has better teeth than me') without looking at the whole story. Becoming more aware of these comparisons will make you realise how unfair and one-sided they are.

Thought Crime 3: Dwelling on the past and worrying about the future

When you dwell on the past or worry about the future all you're doing is wasting time. Ruminating and worrying aggravate your preoccupations with appearance and make you feel rubbish. For example, 'If only I hadn't done that' or 'What if X, Y or Z happens?'

The past has been and gone; unless you have a time machine you can't do anything about it. You can only learn from it and move on – reflect rather than ruminate. Meanwhile, worrying about the future is pointless because you're worrying about something that hasn't happened yet and that probably never will. What you do shapes events, not your thoughts. For example, 'What if he hates my double chin?' This encounter hasn't happened yet so why are you worrying about it? It's just wasting valuable time that could be spent enjoying life! If he does say, 'Wow, I hate your double chin', then you can deal with it, but what are the chances of that happening, really?

Dwelling and worrying shift your mind from focusing on the reality of a situation to things that have either already happened or might never happen so aren't important. They also provoke catastrophising NATs, making you jump to the worst conclusions.

Ⓢ Stop dwelling and worrying

✦ The next time you find yourself worrying about the future ask yourself:
'Can I do anything about it?' If the answer is no then stop worrying and
think about something else. If the answer is yes, then make a plan for
tackling the issue (using the mountain to molehill guide in Chapter 4,
see page 68)

✦ If you can't beat the worries use the 'catastrophising golden rule' from
the last chapter (see page 118), asking yourself, 'What's the worst that
can happen? If it does happen can I cope with it? What's realistically
most likely to happen? And, what's the best thing that can happen?'

✦ The next time you find yourself ruminating on the past use your
feelings as a guide. Ask yourself: 'How do I feel?' If the answer is 'bad',
then stop and distract yourself

Review: You may think that 'worrying' will better prepare you for an event,
but it won't – planning, working, researching and finding solutions to
problems prepare you for an event. All worrying does is slow you down.
And, rather than ruminating, use what's happened in the past as a guide to
the future; don't make it an obstacle. Everyone makes mistakes, but
mistakes don't have to define you. Remember: your catastrophising
thoughts are totally unrealistic 99.9 per cent of the time (and even if the
worst does happen, you'll be able to cope with it).

Thought Crime 4: Secondary agendas

Whatever you're doing, your mind has a two-stage plan for tackling it; an
understanding of both what's happening and what you want to happen:

✦ **Primary agenda:** What you're doing or plan to do

✦ **Secondary agenda:** The expectations, rules and conditions you set
yourself when undertaking your primary agenda that dictate whether
you succeed or fail

Secondary agendas are parameters for success dictated by your inner critic. The belief system you have been nurturing for years will decide how much you expect of yourself and what you consider important and will then lay down rules for achieving these aims. Secondary agendas make you lose focus on your primary agenda – what you're actually doing – and fuel insecurities.

Example: Daisy's dinner date

Daisy's new colleagues invited her out for dinner to welcome her to the team. As she got ready, she thought, 'I have to look sophisticated, but not like I've tried too hard. I can't make any stupid jokes or tell them why I left my old job. I have to remember everyone's names and can only have two glasses of wine so I don't make a fool of myself'.

All night Daisy kept checking in with her secondary agenda to see how she was doing. So much so that she actually missed quite a lot of the conversation and a couple of times had to ask someone to repeat themselves. Also, when everyone else ordered more wine, she ordered a glass of water so she wouldn't break her 'no more than two glasses' rule (even though she quite fancied some more wine). This made her feel selfconscious – would they think she was a kill-joy?

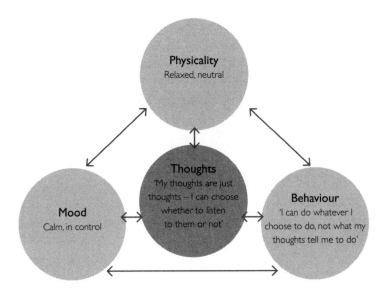

Secondary agendas inspire worry, rumination, insecurity and distraction. They stop you enjoying what you're doing because you're caught up inside your own head and if you break one of the rules you'll feel bad about yourself, dwell on it and then worry about it happening again in the future.

Most of the time you'll accept your secondary agendas without question because there must be some sense in them, right? NO. You already know how biased your mind can be when it comes to you, so you should challenge these protocols and ask yourself, 'Do I really need to follow these?' You can then choose how to proceed and judge whether the rules are worth following. Stop making life difficult for yourself!

Learning compassion

You would never dream of speaking to anyone else the way you speak to yourself. If one of your friends suffered from the same body image anxieties that you do, you'd show them compassion, kindness and warmth – yet you bully, berate and criticise yourself. It's hardly fair, is it? As schmaltzy as it sounds, you need to start being more compassionate towards yourself.

Ⓢ Friendly advice

+ The next time you're feeling down about your appearance ask yourself: 'What would I tell a friend?' or 'What would X say if I ran it past them?' (And make sure X is a reasonable person and not your mortal enemy)
+ Put this advice into action. You're far more likely to be fairer, nicer and kinder to someone else than to yourself, so often the only way to get reasonable advice is to act as if it's not for you

Review: This should give you some distance from sensitive situations so you can get a fairer perspective. Once you've taken the emotional charge out of it, you'll more often than not realise that what you're worrying about isn't that big a deal.

Recognise your achievements

You need to learn how to focus your mental spotlight on your achievements, so the next time you make a mistake you won't beat yourself up about it. At the moment you probably view mistakes as a representation of your rubbishness in general, but everyone makes mistakes. Owning up to them, learning from them and moving on are the traits of a confident, self-assured and self-accepting person.

Here are a couple of examples that illustrate how you probably think at the moment:

A When you eat the cake you were saving:

I'm so disgusting; I have no will power → *now the whole day is ruined* → *eat more cake*

B When you snap at your partner

They're going to be angry with me all day → *I'm such an idiot* → *feel worse*

By giving yourself credit for the things you do well, you'll build your self-esteem and feel stronger, so that when things do go wrong, instead of hating yourself for it you'll dust yourself off and get on with it. Mistakes are a normal part of life. All you have to do is acknowledge them and move on. That's all. If you do that, when you next finish the cake you'll think this way instead:

That didn't fit with the plan → *but it was delicious* → *continue with healthy eating plan*

⑤ Three good things

If you make a mistake or are facing something tough, do the following:

Part 1

A Take a deep breath

B Find some positives: 'That cake was the best I've ever eaten'; 'At least I didn't shout at my boss as well as my partner'

C Make a plan for dealing with the issue, such as continuing with your eating plan as normal or apologising to your partner

Part 2

A For the next week, before you go to bed write down three things you did well during the day. It could be anything: making someone laugh; not checking your compact mirror at all; getting a project in on time (Yes, you have to find three things – it doesn't matter how big or small.)

B At the end of the week read back through your notes

Review: See? You aren't a failure – there are always good and bad sides to everything. For example, you may get made redundant (pretty bad), but at least you're getting a pay-off, have a good CV and you were bored with the job anyway (pretty good). Or you get toothache and discover you must have your wisdom tooth removed (very bad), but at least it happened now and not next month when it's your sister's wedding (great!).

Starting to look for the good in situations and how you cope with tough issues will bolster your self-esteem, which will feed into a healthier, more positive, body image.

Getting out of your head

People with body image issues often view themselves from an observer's perspective – as if they can step back and see themselves as an onlooker in a situation. Unfortunately their anxieties and fears warp what they see, exaggerating their so-called 'flaws' and visualising problems that aren't real or that no one else would be aware of. This is fueled by the belief in Theory A (see pages 32–3), that you do actually have something wrong with you, as well as insecurities from your past, such as being teased at school or having an unflattering nickname. It can also be triggered by a dramatic change in your physicality, such as becoming pregnant or losing/gaining a lot of weight. Your brain fuses this mental image of yourself with reality so you truly see an ugly or defective person when you look at yourself. Even though this view is unrealistic and you have no idea what other people are thinking, you can't shake the image or update it.

Your NATs, secondary agendas, self-criticism and attentional bias can act like quicksand, sucking you in and stopping you from getting where you want to go. Spending all this time in your head can mean that life passes you by ('How is it June already?').

The next strategy was developed by Professor Adrian Wells at University of Manchester. It will teach you how to focus on the moment and get out of your head. The world around you is full of sights, sounds, textures, smells and events that you're missing out on. By focusing on the present moment, you're giving your mind a break. As you become more aware of the world around you, you're becoming less aware of your body image anxieties – giving them less prominence and attention and allowing you to focus on other things. You'll feel more in control, positive about yourself and life in general, and it will stop you viewing yourself from an observer's perspective. It's clever stuff.

Ⓢ Present moment focus training

Starter notes:

+ Put aside 10–15 minutes every day for the next week
+ Every time worries, anxieties, insecurities or secondary agendas pop into your head, acknowledge them and then re-focus on the task at hand (don't get angry with your mind for wandering – that's what it's designed to do)
+ Remind yourself that there's no 'right' or 'wrong' with this exercise. You can't win, pass or fail at it. Everyone's experience is different
+ You won't become an expert at this immediately, it'll take practice. You've spent years and years (if not your entire life) letting your thoughts consume you, so allowing yourself the chance to step back from them will take some getting used to

1 Becoming aware of different sights and sounds

Practising inside:

+ Turn on some music and really listen to it. What instruments are playing? What are the lyrics? Any special effects? Does the pace vary?
+ Alternatively, sit straight-backed on a chair with your feet planted firmly on the floor. Now listen to any sounds you can hear. Is a clock ticking? Is a floorboard creaking? Is the wind howling, birds singing, cars honking?

✦ Next, look around. What colours can you see? Can you name them? Where's the light and shade?

✦ Imagine yourself touching the objects you see. What would they feel like? Rough, smooth, sharp, cold, warm?

Practising outside:

✦ What sounds are all around you? Try to listen out for anything close by – cars, birds, leaves rustling. And then listen out for anything further away – a distant car alarm, a dog barking or a train

✦ What can you see? Buildings, plants, trees, traffic, graffiti, people? What colours can you identify? What patterns and textures?

2 Switching attention between sounds and sights

✦ Pick three of the sounds you can hear to focus on

✦ Channel all your attention onto one of the sounds, letting it fill your awareness completely. If your attention drifts, don't worry, just bring it gently back to the sound

✦ After a minute, shift your attention to the second sound and let it totally absorb you before moving onto the third

✦ Follow the same process for three objects you can see. Let them consume all your attention

3 Pulling it all together

✦ Expand your awareness to take in everything – all of the sights and sounds together. Let them fill your mind with their colour and noise so that you're lost in the outside world

✦ This may take some getting used to, but the more you practise the easier you'll find being present in the moment rather than trapped inside your head

✦ Try it in lots of different situations when you can put aside 10 minutes

– in your office, in the park, walking to work, on the bus. Let your body and mind be consumed with 'out there'

Expand the practice to take in smells, tastes and touch too – incorporating all your senses in the moment. Once you feel more confident with it you can practise during your day-to-day life. For example, while you're having a conversation with someone, focus completely on what they're saying and how they're saying it rather than letting your mind drift to the work you've got to do or what you're having for dinner later.

Fill in this table to monitor your practice:

Day/Date	Situation	What I focused my attention on	Any other comments
Monday	Walking to work	What I could see	I noticed the walk went quicker than usual
Tuesday	Eating my lunch	I tried to eat mindfully	I found it hard to bat away thoughts about all the work I had to do
Wednesday	Listening to music	The lyrics to the songs	I hadn't realised one of the songs I love was about a cat

Review: Re-focusing your mind to encourage awareness of the present moment will take the sting out of painful thoughts and emotions and will stop you getting stuck in your head. Mindfulness is proven to make people feel calmer and more present in what they're doing, so life stops passing them by. It's a wonderful exercise for whenever you find yourself being too self-focused. Simply concentrate on what's around you: the hardness under your feet, the feel of your fingers on your computer keyboard, the sound of the clock ticking over your shoulder.

The pros and cons of being stuck in your head:

Pros	Cons
✦ None	✦ It makes you feel anxious and bad about yourself
Big fat ZERO	✦ You're constantly distracted and miss what's going on around you
	✦ You often have to ask people to repeat themselves or feel you're always one step behind in conversations
	✦ You're overtly self-critical
	✦ You live your life according to secondary agendas, so are always setting yourself up for a 'pass' or 'fail'
	✦ You constantly compare yourself to others and find yourself lacking
	✦ You dwell on and regret the past
	✦ Time zooms past without you feeling you're really experiencing life
	✦ You see yourself as a set of component parts rather than as a whole

Making time for yourself

Schedule in some positive time for yourself – 'me breaks'. Looking after yourself is an important part of feeling good and when you feel good, it's much easier to silence that inner critic. 'Me breaks' are a great way to fill the time that used to be spent indulging bad body image behaviours (which hopefully you're in the process of cutting down/out altogether).

ⓢ 'Me breaks'

✦ Book half an hour in every day for yourself for the next week. Oh, come on – surely half an hour isn't that impossible? Maybe you could set your alarm half an hour early, or cut your pub-time down for a week. (Booking it in is important, otherwise you'll just skip it or forget about it)

✦ Plan what you're going to do during the half hour and then DO IT. We have suggested a list of things that are all relaxing and that will make you feel good, taking your mind off any bad or sad thoughts

Ideas for 'me breaks'

+ Play a game, complete a puzzle
+ Read a book or newspaper
+ Exercise (see Chapter 9)
+ Listen to music
+ Watch your favourite TV programme or film
+ Practise mindfulness
+ Call a friend you haven't spoken to for ages
+ Have a bath (a proven mood-booster)
+ Practise deep breathing (place one hand on your chest, one on your abdomen. Breathe through your nose with your mouth shut. Feel your abdomen expand as you inhale and then deflate as you exhale.)

Review: Booking in time for yourself can feel decadent, but it's an essential part of building self-esteem. Learning to be comfortable in your own company will stop self-recrimination cycles developing and relaxing will make you feel less stressed, less anxious and more in control.

Thoughts to take away

✓ You can shut your inner critic up by focusing on the world around you rather than getting stuck inside your head

✓ Accepting compliments, acknowledging your achievements and seeking a fairer view regarding comparisons will build your self-esteem

✓ Spending positive time on yourself will make you feel calmer, more in control and better able to cope with stress

9

Facing Your Fears

Avoiding something through fear of rejection or failure is a common symptom of body image anxiety. However, avoidance and procrastination only ever make issues seem harder to deal with. In this chapter you'll learn to face your fears, building confidence, self-acceptance and self-esteem.

Avoiding avoidance

Avoidance is like Marmite: it inspires both love and hate. When you're sitting in the cinema elbow-deep in buttery popcorn instead of at home wading through work, you love it. When you stagger into the daylight with no time to start, let alone finish, your work, you hate it. Often, though, the love never materialises because every second spent avoiding something is caught up in worry and guilt.

Body image anxieties can ramp up avoidance tendencies. You're so insecure about your appearance you put off doing things through fear of failure, ridicule or rejection. It can affect every aspect of your life: whether going for a new job, dating, socialising or exercising. Your body image angst has chipped away at your self-esteem so much that, 'I don't look right' has turned into 'I'm not clever, witty, fun or good enough'. This is because you're adhering to Theory A, 'I have a problem with how I look', rather than Theory B, 'I think I have a problem with how I look'. Theory A is nonsense. Your only problem is the way you feel and think about your appearance as you behave in negative ways, feel bad and miss wonderful opportunities.

How you feel about a situation does not indicate how things really are. You may dread something, but that doesn't mean it's going to be dreadful. Have you ever cancelled plans because you're tired and can't be bothered, then thought, 'I probably would have had a good time'? Remember: How you feel at the start of an event doesn't indicate how you'll feel at the end.

Imagining success

When you're worried about doing something, it's natural to imagine all the potential hideous outcomes, like people pointing and laughing at you; falling on your face in front of your colleagues; a waiter refusing to serve you because you're so hideous he can't bear to look at you. Visualising these things inspires the same emotions and physical responses you'd experience if they actually happened: shame, embarrassment, horror, physical tension and nausea. You're making yourself live through a nightmare that hasn't happened and, realistically, never would.

These visualisations inspire the self-fulfilling prophecy behaviour we've discussed before (see page 117) – you've seen it happen in your head so feel the result is inevitable and then act accordingly, for example by self-sabotage: breaking up with someone before they can break up with you. Acting this way means you never prove that you could have succeeded and that things might have turned out differently.

Instead of always imagining the worst possible scenario, start imagining the best. Running through the positive outcomes of an event will make you feel uplifted, confident and excited rather than petrified and defensive. Visualising every detail of a scene or a sporting event is a common technique used by actors and athletes before performing or competing. Such visualising will help you to:

+ Familiarise yourself with all you need to do so you feel well prepared
+ Build your confidence before you do something new
+ Reduce negative thoughts by concentrating on positive outcomes
+ Aim for success because you've already seen and tasted it!

⑤ Visualising success
Think of something you need to face that you've been dreading/avoiding thinking about.

1 Write down the specific issue or situation that's bothering you.
   My boyfriend wants me to meet his parents. I know they'll tell him I'm not good enough for him

2 What is the very best course of events? Note down what you do, what others do and your preferred final result.
   I am very polite, say the right things, have great table manners and make them laugh. They are polite back, compliment me, smile a lot and invite me to stay for coffee

3 Read your statement out loud. Physically hearing the words will lodge them in your mind, make you realise they're not unrealistic and will motivate you to see this through. You may also spot a missing step, something you want to add or an obstacle you need to work round.
If they ask me anything about my previous marriage I'll say, 'I didn't want to spend my life being unhappy' – keep it general and non-specific, but not rude or defensive. Then I'll change the subject

4 Close your eyes, clear your mind and take some deep breaths

5 Now, picture the most confident version of yourself. It's you on your best-ever day. What are you wearing? How are you standing?
I am wearing a bright-red necklace I bought yesterday and my black dress. The red is to remind me not to hide away and that I can be brave. I will stand confidently with my head held high and back straight. I won't cross my arms or bite my nails

6 Stand up and practise this posture/stance. Lower your shoulders, straighten your back, keep your chin up. Smile (skip smiling if you're breaking up with your partner/telling someone you crashed their car)

7 Run through the scene in your head, step by step. What does this confident version of you say, do, think and feel? This is your movie; you're the director and control everything

8 Watch yourself succeed!

Review: Visualisation may seem strange, even ridiculous, at first, but it's proven to increase confidence in tricky situations. Even if things don't go according to plan, you'll be in a better position to deal with the fall-out, as you'll be feeling more self-assured. Whatever happens, you've seen yourself succeed, so you know it's possible.

Testing your doom and gloom theories

Thinking positively and realistically about a situation is the right way to think, however much your inner critic tries to convince you otherwise.

And the only way to start doing that is to test out your doom and gloom theories to scupper them once and for all.

We want you to start facing the situations and scenarios you fear. Avoidance and procrastination are awful because they ramp up anticipatory anxiety – you always feel more anxious before you start something because of the unknowns. Your insecurity makes it into an insurmountable mountain that gets bigger and more terrifying each day you avoid it, whereas by starting to think about it, the mountain deflates into a more manageable hill. Your anxiety will drop as soon as you face your fears. By not entering a situation, or deliberately sabotaging a positive result, you won't get the chance to see that it could have gone well and that your anxieties would naturally drop as you saw it through.

Avoidance versus facing the issue

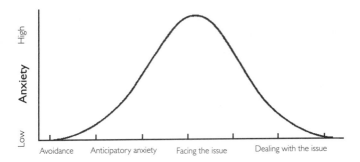

The less you face, the more insecure you'll become (and the more time you'll spend worrying about your appearance), whereas the more you face, the more your confidence will build. Even if things don't go according to plan, the fact you had a go and faced your fears will make you feel stronger, as you'll see that you can cope even when things don't work out.

🄢 Facing your fears

+ Write a list of things you've been avoiding or putting off. Here are some ideas to get you started:

+ Going for a promotion
+ Looking for a new job
+ Going swimming
+ Joining a dating website
+ Not re-touching make-up more than once a day
+ Starting the healthy eating plan

+ Undressing in front of your partner
+ Having sex with your partner
+ Exercising in public
+ Going shopping for new clothes
+ Wearing a new dress/suit
+ Joining a gym

+ Put your list in order of difficulty, easiest down to hardest. Break the bigger tasks down into smaller, more manageable, steps, i.e. 'Going for a promotion' turns into 'Look into available positions, job requirements and skills' and 'Book meeting in with boss'. (Starting on the easy things will give you the confidence to tackle the harder things later on.)
+ Using the table (see opposite), write down your worst-case scenario fears. Make sure this is something you can prove. There's no point writing, 'They'll think I'm stupid' because that's just your NATs trying to read minds. You can't know what someone's thinking, you can only go on what happens – start relying on proof
+ Next, work out an experiment to test your theory
+ Note what actually happened and how you feel about the situation now

Key points to remember:
+ Ensure you give the experiment the best chance of success, otherwise this strategy is a waste of time. There's no point, for example, going on a date and hiding in the toilet. Be fair on yourself and behave confidently, openly and positively
+ Face your fear for long enough that your anxiety has time to subside.

For example, when shopping for new clothes try at least five different shops. If you don't complete the experiment you won't give your nerves a chance to calm down

✦ Use the visualising success strategy (pages 147–8) to boost confidence

✦ Don't cheat. For example when shopping, don't buy a dress you already own in a different colour. This task's about doing things differently

✦ Watch out for NATs. Use the Golden Rules (see pages 117–19) to challenge them if they try to put you off

Situation	I don't want my boyfriend to see the scars on my body

Prediction

What do you think will happen?	⟶	He'll be disgusted by them
How likely do you think it is that it'll happen, on a scale of 0–100%?	⟶	100%
How will you know if it has?	⟶	I'll be able to tell by his face and actions, i.e. whether he wants to continue undressing me or not

Experiment

How can you test the prediction?	⟶	Wear a top that shows the start of the scars on my arms and chest. If this puts him off, I'll know without having to take my top off

Outcome

What actually happened?	⟶	It didn't put him off! He said he thought they were unique and interesting

Conclusion

How do you feel about the situation and your prediction after the test?	⟶	I wish I'd had the confidence to let other people see them sooner. He did stare at them, but in an interested way, not voyeuristically. This made me reassess how others have looked at them – maybe they were just intrigued and not disgusted
Looking back at your original prediction, how likely would you say it is now (0–100%)?	⟶	30%. I still believe some people might not like them, but I actually think many will find them compelling

Review: Use this table (see page 151) whenever you find yourself avoiding something or feeling insecure about how you look and don't ever underestimate your ability to cope if something does go wrong. You'll be surprised by how strong you are. For example, if your boyfriend does react negatively to your scars, ask yourself whether this reflects badly on him or you. (Answer: him!) Also, be honest with yourself if a bad result is down to your own behaviour – did you sabotage the experiment? Sometimes it's easier to blame everything on your appearance as you don't have to take responsibility for your actions, but this will only make you feel worse. Disproving your fears by testing them out will make you feel more in control, happier and, yes, more beautiful.

You can take this strategy one step further if and when you feel confident enough, by pushing the limits of your fear. For example, if you hate your thin hair, deliberately wear it in a style that accentuates any thin patches; if you dislike your stomach, wear an unflattering top that accentuates your belly. Whatever your personal body image pariah is, accentuate it. This will make you realise just how little other people notice these things – so little, in fact, that 99.9 per cent of them won't raise an eyebrow and the one person who does will just think you look a little different, but won't be able to put their finger on why. Worst-case scenario: someone mentions your stomach/hair/spots/chin/ears. What then? Well, you simply tell them it's none of their business and that'll be the end of that. The world won't end – nothing will happen. And you'll feel strong.

Exercise and body image

If you have body image anxieties exercise can be the last thing you feel like doing. Getting hot and sweaty in front of a bunch of buff strangers? No thanks. This is a real Catch-22 situation because exercise is proven to lift mood, build confidence, ease stress and keep your body in good shape. The lethargy and guilt you feel by not exercising will only exacerbate your feelings of insecurity, while the pride and physical boost you get from working out will make you feel physically and emotionally better. Don't worry, we're not talking about running marathons, we're talking about any exercise at all – everything from taking the stairs rather than the lift to getting off the bus a stop early and walking home.

The physical benefits of exercise: Exercise releases endorphins, natural feel-good chemicals that act as analgesics, meaning they diminish your perception of pain. When released by your brain's neurotransmitters they bounce through your body, giving you a natural high. Exercise also releases adrenaline, serotonin and dopamine – 'happy' chemicals that work together to make you feel good. Getting your blood pumping strengthens your heart, lungs and muscles and there's a correlation between regular exercise and a reduced risk of heart disease, diabetes and certain cancers. It also burns calories at a faster rate, keeping you at a healthy weight (as long as you eat enough when you're hungry to make up the spent energy).

The emotional benefits of exercise: Where do we start? Not only do you feel good about being proactive, but it's a proven stress-reducer. You're making time for yourself where you can calm down and either think things through or give your mind a break. Exercise has been shown to be as helpful in reducing symptoms of depression as antidepressants and individual and group psychotherapy; research has found your mood lifts just ten minutes after you start exercising. Participants in a study monitoring exercise and depression walked certain distances daily for seven weeks and all of them still reported improved mood and vigour five months after the trial.

Exercise is a wonderful way to gain positive experience of your body. You learn how it works, moves and responds to exertion. It's an easy way to feel more beautiful. A study in the *Journal of Health Psychology* reports that both men's and women's body image improves after just two weeks of moderate exercise, even if no physical change has occurred. And the best bit? There are no rules or regulations for what constitutes worthwhile exercise. As long as your blood's pumping a bit faster and your breath's coming quicker it's beneficial.

Going green

A 2012 survey by mental health charity MIND found that nine out of ten women aged over 30 battle body confidence and low self-esteem when considering outdoor exercise, which is a shame because a whopping 94 per cent of people in a similar survey said 'green exercise' improved their sense of wellbeing. By being too scared to exercise outdoors, you're missing a guaranteed mood-boost. Fresh air and the sights, sounds and experiences of being outside stimulate your body and mind; you're not just stuck in a gym staring at the wall. If you're intimidated by the thought of 'going green', start by walking around the local park with either your iPod or mates for company. Don't let body image anxieties keep you inside.

We want you to start planning exercise into your week (by writing it in your diary you're less likely to skip it). If you don't exercise at the moment, then start gradually. There's no point writing, 'Go to gym Monday, Tuesday, Wednesday and Friday' if you haven't been for six years. You won't manage it and will feel bad about not going. Instead, find something you enjoy that's realistic and achievable. Then, when you've built up your confidence, you can move on to a more formal regime.

Ⓢ Your totally non-intimidating exercise plan

Book what we're calling 'informal' exercises into every single day next week – things that are easily incorporated into your daily life. Here are some suggestions:

+ Get off the train/bus a stop early and walk home
+ Walk up the stairs rather than take the lift
+ Go out dancing with your friends
+ Make housework more energetic, such as dancing while hoovering
+ Do some gardening
+ Walk around the block to get to the sandwich shop at lunchtime
+ Stop taking the car for journeys under one mile
+ Buy, borrow or hire a bike and cycle to work

Ⓢ Your more formal 'I'm taking this seriously' plan

When you're feeling more confident about making changes, book more 'formal' exercise sessions into your diary. Just one or two a week to start with (on top of your daily 'informal' additions). Some suggestions:

+ Join an exercise class. Ask a friend to come along for moral support. You'll be less likely to cancel if you'll be letting someone else down. In classes there's an 'all in it together' mentality, increasing motivation
+ Look into 10-minute exercise regimes or HIT (high-intensity interval training); short, sharp bursts of activity several times a week
+ Buy an exercise DVD and book in a slot to do it twice a week
+ Schedule in a half-hour brisk walk or jog purely for exercise (that is, when you're not running an errand)
+ Join a gym
+ Consider booking a personal trainer
+ Go swimming
+ Join a sports team (this may sound terrifying, but the scariest bit will be signing up – your anxiety will decrease once you've taken the first step)
+ Take up yoga or Pilates (both greatly beneficial to body and mind)
+ Consider exercises that aren't purely about getting fit, but more about enjoying your body and having fun, such as dancing, netball, football, hockey or cycling with friends

✦ Don't let how you feel before you start exercising put you off. Generally you won't feel like it (it's much easier to watch TV, especially if the weather is bad), but remember: how you feel before exercising will bear no resemblance to how you'll feel afterwards. Ask yourself, 'How will I feel if I don't do it?' Regretful and guilty, right? So do it!

✦ Problem-solve any obstacles that might get in the way, such as a fear of being judged by other people. One solution would be to ask a friend along for moral support, but the best solution is to think, 'Who cares what other people think?' Hopefully by this stage in the process you're beginning to believe us when we say everyone's too wrapped up in themselves to care what you look like. People will want to help or join in, that's all. For example, gym instructors will want to give you the best workout and teammates will want to give you tips. No one will ever judge you negatively for exercising – it's positive and life-affirming

Review: Both informal and formal exercises will give you a better appreciation of your body. Give these new regimes a real shot for a month and we're convinced you'll feel better both mentally and physically. You need to learn how to enjoy your body so that you're not exercising because you feel you have to or to lose weight, but because it makes you feel strong, energised and peaceful.

🄢 Your post-exercise mind map

✦ Fill in a mind map after one instance of either informal or formal exercise, noting down how you felt emotionally, physically and what your thoughts were

✦ Be really honest about how you felt. If you didn't feel great, ask yourself why: did you worry about how you looked the whole time you were jogging? Did you deliberately not try during your exercise class and resent everyone else who did?

We have filled out an example mind map to get you started:

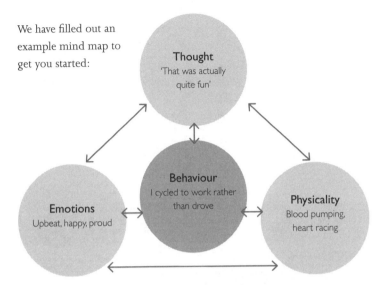

Thought
'That was actually quite fun'

Behaviour
I cycled to work rather than drove

Emotions
Upbeat, happy, proud

Physicality
Blood pumping, heart racing

Thoughts to take away

✓ Avoidance isn't a solution. It only makes things seem more insurmountable and adds guilt, fear and frustration into the mix

✓ Your anxiety will drop as soon as you start facing your fears (just thinking about facing them will make you feel better)

✓ Exercise is a guaranteed way of giving you a healthier and happier body and body image

10

Kick-Starting
Your Life

Now it's time to reassess your core values and make achievable and worthwhile goals to work towards. If you keep acting in positive, life-affirming ways your beliefs about yourself will change and you'll feel more beautiful.

Stop putting your life on hold

Hopefully by now you're giving more credence to the fact that it's not your appearance that's flawed; it's how you feel about it that's flawed. That's okay; you can change how you feel about it!

We've discussed how body image anxieties are both triggered and maintained, how they make you feel emotionally and physically, and how they make you behave. Hiding behind the belief that you are physically flawed (Theory A, see pages 32–3) can create and mask deeper insecurities, which are then never challenged. This book will have brought some of these habits to light so you're more aware of falling back into 'safe' modes of thinking, such as blaming your appearance for holding you back, basing your definitions of happiness on how you look and constantly moving the goalposts for physical 'success'. It can feel reassuring to think about a perceived flaw as it starts a predictable thought, behavioural and emotional process that you've come to know. However, it's this process that's flawed, not your body. Facing your fears and thinking about yourself in fairer, more realistic and positive ways are the only routes to feeling beautiful.

Self-esteem: what is it and how do you get some?

Your self-esteem is self-respect and faith in yourself built on:
+ **Self-assurance:** believing in the validity of your opinions
+ **Self-acceptance:** knowing who you are and accepting yourself as you are
+ **Self-belief:** believing you can achieve what you set out to and can cope if things go wrong

Ask yourself this: 'Would I ever teach children to value themselves according to the way they look?' Hopefully, your answer is no – so why do you follow this philosophy yourself? Why do you rate appearance more highly than you do opinions, values, skills and achievements? You may not like to admit you do, but if your looks dictate how you act, think and feel then that's exactly what's happening. Your self-esteem is measured on what you see as your physical flaws and that needs to change. You need to foster a new measure of self-worth, taking in all your traits, characteristics, achievements, skills and values. The same things you attribute to your friends you need to start attributing to yourself. You're not a set of parts with one thing of more value that the others; you're a complete, whole person.

Now consider what gives your life meaning. What values mean more to you than attractiveness? Your life now is so caught up in looks that these values are getting shunted out without you realising it. It's time to bring them to the forefront of your mind as these are the things that will give you drive, motivation, inspiration, fulfilment and integrity. Reassessing what you find important will make you more determined to change.

Ⓢ Areas of value

There are two parts to this strategy.

Part 1

+ Write these five headings on different pages in your notebook: relationships; work, education/training; free time; spirituality; health
+ For each question in the following table (see overleaf) consider how you wish to act going forward – what values you, well, value in each category and what direction they may take you in. For example, you value kindness and so hope to be a good member of the community
+ Jot down anything that comes to mind, even if it seems stupid. Think of what you would value if you weren't held back by how you feel about your appearance and if you weren't scared of failure or judgement
+ Write what you actually value, not what you think you should value
+ If the questions do not apply to you, leave the section blank
+ After a week, revisit your list and add more values as you think of them

Use the list of values on page 164 to inspire you.

This table is based on the Valued Living Questionnaire from *Acceptance and Commitment Therapy* (Guilford Press, 2004) by Steven C. Hayes, Kirk D. Strosahl and Kelly G. Wilson.

Category	Values
Relationships	**Family:** How do you want to act as a sibling/son/daughter/parent/cousin/ niece/nephew? **Social:** How do you want to act as a friend? How would you like your friends to describe you? How would you like them to think of you? What sort of friend do you want to be? **Romantic:** What sort of partner do you want to be? If you are not in a relationship at present, how would you like to act in a relationship? **Example values:** Caring, kind, compassionate, loyal, dependable, honest, generous, forgiving, fair, humorous, popular, humble **Example value directions:** 'I'd like to be a great parent, a loyal friend, a loving partner'
Work, education and training	What kind of employee, employer or student do you want to be? What values do you appreciate in your staff, colleagues or peers? Are there any areas in which you wish to pursue further education or training? How do you value your work or studies? **Example values:** Commitment, honesty, responsibility, respect, tolerance, success, risk-taking **Example value directions:** 'I'd like to be a committed employee, a respectful student'
Free time	What values do you want to shape your free time? Are there any hobbies, sports or interests that you would like to pursue? What would you like to do for the wider community, e.g. voluntary or charity work, political activity? **Example values:** Fun, humour, independence, knowledge, achievement **Example value directions:** 'I'd like to be a responsible member of the community, a fun member of my football team'
Spirituality	If you're spiritual, what guiding principles mean a lot to you? If you're not, would you like to be? **Example values:** Inner strength, humility, self-control, virtue **Example value directions:** 'I'd like to strive for peace and positivity in my life'

Category	Values
Health	What's important to you in how you care for your physical/mental health? **Example values:** To be fit, compassionate, caring, attractive **Example value directions:** 'I'm going to try to maintain perspective, nurture my self-esteem and respect myself'

Part 2

Next, draw a pie chart representing the five values or value directions you want to guide your life. Physical attractiveness can still be one of them, of course, but ask yourself, 'Do I want it to be my main guiding force in life?' We have filled out an example:

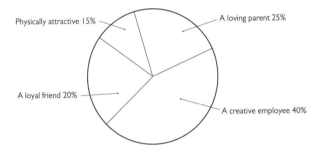

Review: Hopefully this strategy made you realise how many other things there are to focus on and to treasure in yourself and other people than your appearance. Use your pie chart as an approximate guide to how you want to live your life at the moment. Picking five doesn't mean you disregard other values; it's just a way of keeping things on track and focusing on what's important to you at this particular time. You can update it as and when your priorities change (perhaps 'attractiveness' will drop out of your top five altogether sooner than you think).

List of values

Acceptance: to feel accepted among my peers

Achievement: to achieve what I set out to

Ambition: to always strive to better myself

Attractiveness: to look after my personal appearance

Caring: to always take other people's feelings and circumstances into consideration

Compassion: to feel concern for others and myself

Confidence: to have faith in my own skills and abilities

Courtesy: to be polite and considerate to others

Creativity: to have original ideas

Dependability: to be reliable and trustworthy

Fairness: to be fair to myself and to others

Family: to have a happy, loving family

Flexibility: to adjust to new or unusual situations easily

Friendliness: to have close and supportive friends and to be considered friendly to others

Fun: to be considered good company and to take time out to enjoy myself

Generosity: to give what I can to others

Health: to be physically well and healthy

Honesty: to be truthful and genuine

Humility: to be modest and not unnecessarily self-promoting

Humour: to always try to see the funny side

Independence: to trust myself and my decision-making abilities

Justice: to make sure I promote equal and fair treatment to others whenever I can

Knowledge: to never stop learning

Love: to be loved by those close to me and to love others

Loyalty: to be considered reliable and trustworthy

Popularity: to be well liked by many people

Power: to have control over others

Realism: to see things realistically and in as objective a way as possible

Religion: to follow the teachings of my chosen religion

Respect: to have people respect, trust and look up to me and to respect, trust and look up to other people

Responsibility: to make and carry out important decisions to the best of my ability and knowledge

Risk: to take risks and make the most of opportunities that come my way

Safety: to be safe and secure in what I think and what I do

Self-control: to be disciplined and govern my own actions

Self-esteem: to like myself, just as I am

Self-knowledge: to have a deep, honest understanding of myself

Sexuality: to have an active and satisfying sex life

Spirituality: to grow spiritually

Strength: to be physically strong and/or to nurture an inner strength

Success: to achieve everything I set out to, or at least give it a try

Tolerance: to accept and respect those different from me

Virtue: to live a good, moral life

Wealth: to have as much money as I need

Making meaningful goals

Most people with body image anxieties make goals around appearance, such as, 'I'll lose a stone, then I'll be happier'. We're constantly told via the media that changing our appearance will change our lives, but it will only change your appearance. The only way to fundamentally change your life for the better is to learn self-acceptance and improve self-esteem so you can grab opportunities. Working towards goals that give your life meaning and direction will give you hope for the future, take your mind off your appearance and give you a sense of achievement and fulfilment.

Ⓢ Goal planning

Part 1

Write down things you've always wanted to do (nothing is too big or too small). Things you either dismissed because you thought you were too ugly, fat, thin, bald or grey to do them, or that you put on hold until you 'fixed' your appearance. If you're struggling, ask yourself:

+ If I looked like I do in my dreams what would my job be?
+ If I lost that stone what would I go and do?
+ What did I stop doing because I felt insecure?
+ What do I miss doing?
+ What do I envy my friends doing?
+ What aren't I doing now because I'm worried about my appearance?
+ What was the last thing I said I'd do 'when I looked right'?

Some ideas: Starting a creative writing course, going travelling, starting online dating, starting an evening class, going swimming again, doing charity work, finding a dream job, coaching football, joining a sports team, cycling to work, going dancing, booking a beach holiday, getting in touch with old friends, letting people take photos of me.

Part 2

✦ Break your ideas down into short-term (1 month), medium-term (6 months) and long-term goals (1–5 years). Don't dismiss any. For more ambitious goals, break them into manageable parts. For 'become a pilot', write down 'look into piloting schools' on your short-term list.

✦ Make sure your goals are S.M.A.R.T:

  ✦ **Specific:** What exactly is your goal? How would things be different if you achieved it? Example: 'I'll cycle to work every day next week to get some exercise and feel good about being proactive'

  ✦ **Measurable:** It has to be something that's quantifiable so you know when you've achieved it, for example, not 'I will get my dream job', more, 'I will apply for that job I saw in sales'

  ✦ **Attainable:** It has to be something you can realistically achieve, such as, 'I will sign up to a creative writing course in a month's time,' rather than, 'I will write a bestselling novel in a month's time'

  ✦ **Relevant:** The goal has to be worthwhile. If you won't feel any joy in it then it's pointless. It has to mean something to you or you'll put off trying. Remember: perfection doesn't exist. This exercise isn't about striving for a mythological ideal – by accepting nothing less, you'll never give yourself credit for what you do achieve

  ✦ **Time-specific:** Stick to the short-, medium- and long-term timelines. Don't just vaguely say, 'I'll do something nice next month'

✦ Here are some ideas to get you thinking:

Short-term (1 month):

  ✦ Start exercising both informally and formally every week
  ✦ Keep to the healthy eating plan
  ✦ Keep a tab on all unhelpful body-control behaviours

Medium-term (6 months)

  ✦ Challenge all my NATs, so I start seeing things more realistically
  ✦ Speak to my boss about a possible promotion

+ Take steps to tackle an on-going problem (such as a miserable job)

Long-term (1–5 years)

+ Go to university or study in the evenings
+ Learn a new language
+ Go travelling

Part 3

+ Book times/dates when you're going to start investigating new jobs or join a cookery school, for example. Otherwise, you won't do it
+ Work around any self-sabotaging tendencies, NATs or potential barriers so nothing gets in your way. Test out the fear like you did in Chapter 9 (if you need to). Don't tell yourself you haven't got time – this is a priority! Delegate or get rid of things you don't enjoy or don't need to do. Also, consider asking a friend to join you as social support is a big self-esteem booster and you'll feel less likely to cancel/duck out

Review: Taking your goals seriously will make you feel excited, interested in life and more in control. Don't write anything off, be realistic and make sure the goals are achievable. So if you want to become a movie star but haven't acted before, start by looking up local acting classes.

Example: Tailor-made

Lewis had always wanted to be a tailor, but his school friends had laughed at him and he'd carried the idea that this dream was embarrassing into adulthood. This fear had been accentuated by the fact that he had acne. He thought, 'No one in the fashion industry is spotty, why would they accept me?' Now he had a joyless 9–5 job and couldn't stop thinking about what he'd rather be doing. He put 'look into tailoring courses' on his short-term goal list and booked it in. When the time arrived, he considered skipping it   ⋯⋮⋅

⋯⟶ ('Why make myself feel worse?') but he found an evening course starting in six months' time. It was pricey, but the way his heart leapt when he saw the course convinced him to enquire about a payment plan, which he followed up. Lewis felt a weight lift off his shoulders. Even if this course didn't work out, the fact that he'd taken those first steps convinced him it was a possibility.

Lewis' mind map looks like this:

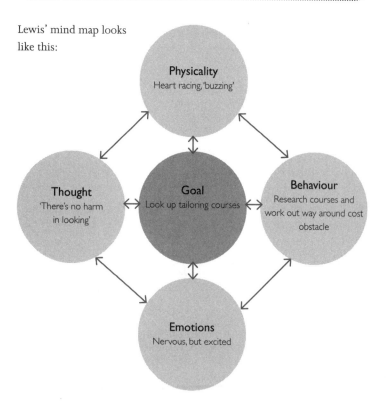

A beautiful belief

Humans like things to make sense and to fit together nicely. This is why prejudice is such a pain to shift: if you truly believe that something is a certain way, you'll ignore all evidence to the contrary. For example, if you believe aliens landed in your backyard, you'll hunt out everything that proves it ('Look at those scorch marks in a perfect circle on the lawn!') and dismiss anything or anyone that says otherwise ('Aren't those marks from the BBQ we had last night?'). People want consistency and have an internal need for all their beliefs to be harmonious. This means that when two beliefs conflict we feel uncomfortable and change one of our views to fit with the other ('cognitive dissonance').

So far your beliefs have been all 'I'm ugly/rubbish/too spotty', but in working through this book hopefully you're beginning to act in ways that contradict these thoughts. This might feel uncomfortable – how can beliefs you've held about yourself have been wrong all this time? However, if you continue to behave in ways that disprove your body image anxieties, research into cognitive dissonance proves you'll eventually change your beliefs to back up this new evidence – keep doing what you're doing and you'll eventually believe you look beautiful just as you are.

Ⓢ Truly feeling beautiful

Step 1

Write a letter to a young person you know is suffering from body image anxieties – a daughter/son, friend, or yourself right now or two/five/ten/twenty years ago. Write about your experience of being preoccupied with your looks and the emotional/physical costs of pursuing a nonsense 'beauty ideal'. Include the amount of time taken up with feeling bad about yourself, the things you missed, the times you felt low, how body-control behaviours you indulged in made you feel, how comparing yourself to anyone based on appearance isn't fair on you or them. Be totally honest.

Example: Kirsten's letter

Dear younger Kirsten,

Unless you change how you feel about your appearance now, you're going to spend the next ten years caught up in a cycle of horribleness. You'll be so fixated on how you look you'll miss out on amazing opportunities and experiences. You'll say no to Steven when he asks you to the school prom and you'll regret it for years. You only say no because you're scared of wearing a dress that shows your arms, but you'll soon realise he wouldn't have asked you if he didn't like you just as you were. He'll go with Amanda instead and you'll resent her for it, although it's not her fault. Please go and have an amazing time and trust in what he tells you, rather than in what you believe.

You'll spend your late teens avoiding photographs, which is a huge shame because you have no record of brilliant holidays with friends, and in ten years you'll look back on the few snaps you do have and realise how lovely you looked. You'll also spend hours looking at famous people online, ignoring the great things you have, focusing instead on what they have that you want. It's painful and pointless. You'll comfort eat, but it won't comfort you, it'll make you feel worse – emotionally and physically. I've finally accepted how I look (yes, even my 'wrestler's arms') and, brace yourself, I even like it. So embrace what you have and enjoy your life because it goes by so fast.

Good luck! Older (and wiser) Kirsten

Step 2

Broaden your perspective about health and beauty. Read more books about body image and Google fine art images, modern art and photographers who specialise in the human form. This is a guaranteed way of getting an unbiased take on beauty. Art doesn't exist to market a product, so isn't intended to leave you feeling inadequate or anxious. It's designed to celebrate all shapes and sizes from different cultural perspectives. You've had tunnel vision where beauty is concerned for so long you've lost perspective: everyone looks different and there isn't a 'right' way to look.

Step 3

Recognise that appearance prejudice is a form of discrimination, the same as any other. Any assumption that the way someone (including you) looks is a good indicator of character, morality, intelligence or success is incorrect and unjust. Don't judge a book by its cover.

Please sign your anti-discrimination pledge below:

I, _____, do solemnly declare I will no longer be prejudiced against myself or others based on appearance. I will endeavour to appreciate people (or dislike them – let's be honest, some people are not very nice) based upon what they're like as a whole person (rather than a collection of physical parts).

Thoughts to take away

✓ Identifying the values you hold dear will guide you in how you want to live your life and reassure you that you're not defined by your appearance

✓ Making achievable and worthwhile goals will give you direction and inspire you to move forward and feel excited about life

✓ The more you act in positive ways, the more beautiful you'll feel

A final message

Congratulations! You've worked your way through some pretty tough strategies to reach this point, so a pat on the back is in order. Body image anxieties can make life a slog, but it's genuinely not your appearance that's holding you back, it's how you feel about your appearance. Once you start questioning those feelings and chipping away at the prejudice you hold against yourself, you'll realise that physical attractiveness is a tiny part of a massive picture: you're so much more than how you look.

Hopefully you're feeling more beautiful than you've felt for a long time, channelling a new attitude of self-acceptance and confidence. We're crossing our fingers that you're thinking about yourself in a much more balanced, realistic way than you were before. Changing negative beliefs about yourself is an on-going process and will take time. There's no quick fix, so don't panic if you're not feeling beautiful yet – if you even feel a tiny bit more self-assured that's something to celebrate. Recognising that thoughts aren't facts and that your behaviour might have been aggravating insecurities is half the battle. Keep on practising the strategies until they become second nature and your self-esteem will keep climbing.

If you feel more positive about yourself and have faith things can change then it's time for some air-punching, because that's amazing. Making changes will have been incredibly hard and will continue to be, but recognising how far you've come is a big deal. To measure how you're feeling about things now, please answer these questions:

1 **After reading the book – how do you feel?**

   A The same – no change

   B A little better – starting to think this all through

   C Better – putting improvements in place

   D Amazing – transformed

If you answered option A, did you really put all your energy into the strategies? Are you willing to try them again? If you're still struggling and the book hasn't helped as much as you'd hoped then we suggest speaking to your GP, who'll be able to recommend further treatment. There are also some useful websites and resources at the back of the book.

If you answered B–D then we salute you. Things will only get better if you continue putting what you've learned into practice.

2 **Which of the 'thoughts to take away' at the end of the chapters particularly struck a chord?** Write them in your notepad so that every time you need a pick-me-up you can flick back to motivate yourself.

3 **What support network do you have available to help maintain what you've learned?** Social support is a crucial motivator. Consider telling family and friends what you're doing. Their encouragement will be invaluable and talking through things will allow you to get a different perspective. It might also show you the funny side. Laughter is a proven mood-booster and will make you feel better able to cope.

4 **What potential obstacles might throw you off course?** Write them down and work through any possible solutions.

5 **Go back through the symptom check list in Chapter 2 and tick the boxes that apply to you now. How does the list compare to the one you did originally?** Hopefully there will be fewer ticked! For any symptoms you're still experiencing go through the book again to the relevant chapters and re-work the strategies until you feel confident you can beat them.

6 **Are you going to stop unhelpful behaviours that only serve to perpetuate your insecurities?**

7 **Are you going to be more aware of your emotional triggers and try to behave in ways that will lift your mood rather than aggravate it?** Remember: your mood doesn't have to dictate your day.

8 **Are you going to foster a healthy approach to eating so you feel both physically and emotionally energised?**

9 **Are you going to challenge NATs and your inner critic and start being more realistic and fair on yourself?**

10 **When are you going to start thinking differently?**

   A 'I already have'

   B 'Today'

   C 'Next week'

   D 'Next year'

   E 'I don't care'

These questions aren't meant to trip you up – there are no right or wrong answers. They're merely a means to assess how you feel now and if there are any specific areas you want to concentrate on. You now have the tools to feel beautiful – how you use them is up to you. One of this book's overarching messages is that you have choices. You can choose to feel better about yourself, to accept your appearance and to work towards exciting goals. Change is hard, but it's rewarding. And it works. There will be times when you question yourself – that's normal – but now you know how to navigate those blips you can manage whatever life throws at you.

If there are some bits of the book that you haven't tackled yet, go back and try again, reminding yourself what you're meant to be doing and why. Look over the 'Why do I want to feel beautiful?' list you made in Chapter 1 (see page 22) and think of how wonderful you'll feel by tackling the thoughts, behaviours and feelings that are holding you back. Often just considering doing things differently is the hardest bit, but by reading this book you've already passed that stage. Don't pressurise yourself to change overnight. Make a date to re-read the book in a month, six months or a year's time to see how differently you feel then and keep the ideas fresh in your mind. Don't let life pass you by while you decide whether you want to live it. By fostering an attitude of self-acceptance and by appreciating all your good bits – you'll feel beautiful.

Further reading

David Veale, Rob Wilson and Alex Clarke, *Overcoming Body Image Problems including Body Dysmorphic Disorder* (Robinson, 2009)

Susie Orbach, *Susie Orbach on Eating: Change your eating, change your life* (Penguin Books, 2002)

Dennis Greenberger and Christine A. Padesky, *Mind over Mood: A cognitive treatment manual for clients* (Guilford Press, 1995)

David O. Burns, *The Feeling Good Handbook* (William Morrow, 2000)

Useful websites

MIND, The National Association for Mental Health: www.mind.org.uk/

Time to Change: www.time-to-change.org.uk

Body Acceptance: www.cci.health.wa.gov.au/resources/infopax.cfm?Info_ID=55

Be Mindful: www.bemindful.co.uk

Mood Gym: www.moodgym.anu.edu.au

Living Life to the Full: www.llttf.com

The Centre for Clinical Interventions: www.cci.health.wa.gov.au

The Mental Health Foundation: www.mentalhealth.org.uk

The American Mental Health Foundation: www.americanmentalhealthfoundation.org

The Beck Institute: www.beckinstitute.org

Cruse Bereavement Care: www.cruse.org.uk

Relate: www.relate.org.uk

Frank, friendly confidential drugs advice: www.talktofrank.com

Alcohol Concern: www.alcoholconcern.org.uk

The British Psychological Society: www.bps.org.uk

The British Association for Behavioural & Cognitive Psychotherapy: www.babcp.com

Samaritans: www.samaritans.org

Acknowledgements

We have so much gratitude for everyone who believed in these books and helped to make them happen. A huge thanks to our wonderful families, especially Ben, Jack, Max and Edie. Also to dietician Carole Bower for her advice and support, biology teacher extraordinaire Michael Smyth for his scientific know-how, Kerry Enzor and Richard Green at Quercus for their unfaltering enthusiasm, our agent Jane Graham Maw for her encouragement, and Jo Godfrey Wood and Peggy Sadler at Bookworx for their unsurpassed editing and design skills.

References

Chapter 6 eating plan adapted from: Susie Orbach, *Fat is a Feminist Issue: The self-help guide for compulsive eaters* (Arrow Books, 1988)

Chapter 10 list of values table adapted from the Valued Living Questionnaire, Steven C. Hayes, Kirk D. Strosahl and Kelly G. Wilson in *Acceptance and Commitment Therapy* (Guilford Press, 2004)